Can I Have A Word?

To

Vivienne

With Love & Best Wishes

[signature]

Endorsements

Sue has put together such a simple but effective set of techniques to deal with the difficult situations we face as leaders. I have used many of them over challenging times seen in recent years. Sue has a unique style which helps people not only learn the simple techniques, but encourages action, resulting in some incredible impacts.

Chris Brindley MBE
Chair of Rugby League World Cup 2021

Can I have a word? Five simple words strung together that can create that sinking feeling in the pit of your stomach. I've been on the receiving end many times and also used them without even considering the impact on the recipient.

Sue has managed to look at the implications of these words and the conversations around them. Using Vivi as the main character, and amusing cartoon images, Sue introduces six simple techniques to approach difficult conversations in a different way.

If only I'd thought about the impact those five words can have. This book is an essential read for leaders to really think about their communication with their team members and turn those difficult conversations into positive experiences for all.

Sandra Garlick MBE, Founder of Woman Who

Communication is fundamental to every aspect of our lives and yet we often don't do it well, hurting people along the way and making us less likely to achieve our goals. Sue's book provides easy and effective ways to turn what could be a difficult conversation into a developmental opportunity for all the parties involved. Her approach works not just in the workplace but also at home with your partner or your teenage children. All I can say is I wish she had written it sooner!

Dr Elena Liquete, Senior HR Professional.

Can I Have A Word?

Sue...Sue Tonks

Publications

Published: November 2022 Ladey Adey Publications, Ancaster, Lincolnshire UK.

ISBN: 978-1-913579-49-4 (Paperback).

ISBN: 978-1-913579-50-0 (E-Publication).

British Library Cataloguing-in-Publication Data.
A catalogue record for this book is available from The British Library.

Cover Design by Abbirose Adey, of Ladey Adey Publications.

Cartoons by Chris Ryder, Witty Pics Ltd.

Photographs: John Cleary Brand Photography.

If you have enjoyed this book please give a review on Amazon for Sue...Sue Tonks.

Dedication

This book is written in dedication to all the Directors, Managers and Supervisors, who, as delegates on my training programmes, enabled me to develop and perfect my ideas and beliefs on dealing with difficult situations.

To my fabulous wife Susan who has patiently listened to me for years saying; "I would like to write all of this in a book". Thank you for your encouragement, help, support and love. I could never do the things I do without you.

Well Susan, here it is.

Sue...Sue Tonks

About the Author

Sue...Sue Tonks loves approaching life differently.

With her creative and pragmatic mind and the experience she has had across seven industry sectors Sue is ever eager to find easy solutions to everyday problems both inside the workplace and in life.

Her Joint Honours Degree in Psychology and Sociology created a curiosity about human behaviour followed by her baptism of fire as Sue, at the age of 22, managed 86 heavy goods vehicle drivers and fitting staff in her first business role. She was the first female management trainee with British Road Services (BRS) - an interesting start to a lifetime of learning management skills from the bottom up.

Sue realised that there was more to management than a job title. She started to experiment with practical and simple ways to get the best from her team.

During her successful time, in national roles within *BRS, Roadline* and *Group 4 Securitas,* Sue, a fervent learner embarked on and paid her own fees to attend several *Dale Carnegie Management* programmes. This gifted her the understanding of human behaviour principles - many of which are used in this book. She then progressed to become a Dale Carnegie Instructor for 16 years.

Following several senior positions in the civil service and in tour operations with *Airtours* and *Airtours International Airline*, Sue had amassed enough experience to develop her own Leadership and Management training programmes. Today, Sue trains managers at all levels to become effective leaders using her own memorable, highly practical, easy to learn and extraordinary style.

Sue delivers keynotes and workshops with unforgettable comedy moments. Her knowledge and tips on how to get the best from your people, networking and business planning have given her international acclaim. Her fun and practical approach enables delegates to vividly remember key points and develop long lasting skills.

Sue, living in Warwickshire with her wife - also called Sue, is an internationally renowned keynote speaker and trainer on Networking and Leadership. Sue is always busy spreading her skills and techniques to global businesses schools and universities and to manufacturing, accountancy and law firms.

Sue is also the inventor and manufacturer

of multi-award winning *Hydroveg Kits* a sustainable way to grow veg at home in little space with little watering. Sue's plans are to help feed the world.... in addition to running five other businesses! www.hydroveg.co.uk

Sue is also delighted to be the Regional Chair for the Federation of Small Businesses (FSB) in the West Midlands. The FSB is very special to Sue for the amount of support it gives to small businesses, she is honoured to be able to give back. Sue is also on the Warwickshire committee for the Queens Award for Enterprise. How does she find time?

Sue recently realised that she has Dyslexia and Dyscalculia. Although these difficulties must have been with her all her life it never stopped her achievements. With this in mind, she decided to assist her readers, using various tools to aid reading, understanding, learning and retention. She would, wouldn't she?

If Sue can do anything - she can take a problem, find a quick and easy solution and share it with others, just like she is sharing with you today.

For more information about keynotes and training opportunities for your organisation contact Sue at sue@suetonks.com or visit her website www.suetonks.com

Can I Have A Word?

Contents

SIx Techniques

Preface

Years have taught me at least one thing and that is not to try to avoid an unpleasant fact, but rather to grasp it firmly and let the other person observe that I am at least trying to treat him fairly. Then he, it has been my observation, will treat me in the same spirit.

Benjamin Franklin

Richard Tyler

Foreword

We are deep in the midst of some of the most testing and traumatic systems change that most of us will ever had to have lived through. We don't need to look far to see education, political, health and social systems collapsing. On the back of a global pandemic, it seems we are all being forced to look at our own worlds through a new lens. Maybe, this is with *bi-focal vision*. Whilst we need to look at what is immediate and right in front of us, we can perhaps afford to lift our gaze. When we do so we can, in the distance, make out somewhat blurry images of possibility and potential. The lens allows us to focus on what it is we are able to shape ourselves. Maybe this is our opportunity to birth a new world. For so long now, we have looked to those around us to fix our problems and make our spaces better. When they do so, we applaud them. When they fail us, we boo and jeer.

I'm not saying we should let those who are charged with leading our systems, off the hook. No, not at all. What I am suggesting is we each start to look at the places where we can play our own part in leading the way. The small choices we make at home, in our communities and in our organisations, help to model the world we wish to live in. There is a simple equation which goes like this, *if you were to take two parallel train tracks and shift one of them by just one degree, 50 miles down the line, the two tracks would be over a mile apart.*

Incredible. Maybe it suggests to us if we each make small, one degree adaptations to how we live, lead, love and work, we could ignite huge swathes of change.

The first step to this is awareness; starting to notice how you show up. Only with awareness and insight, can you begin to make conscious habit changes. And habit changes require consistency and perseverance. New habits are rarely installed overnight. They can take months.

What I love about Sue's book is it not only does she help you to begin your own adventure of awareness, **she opens up a magic box of gifts** which will support you to define and build in your own new habits. She brings this to you with a fresh air of humour and playfulness and, in a world which has become so entrenched in its serious issues, establishing a sense of play, feels vital.

The new world which we collectively start to architect and then build, will need to have its foundation, firmly in some core values; *trust, truth, compassion, inclusion, discernment* and *kindness.* For any of these values to be lived, we must first all listen and hear what is going on in our own world.

Sue's book has helped remind me as to the importance of truly listening and paying attention, to each other and to ourselves. My suggestion? Devour this book. Start listening and noticing more. Find the habit in here which resonates with you most. Start practising it and see what occurs. Be consistent. Adapt by one degree each time. Who knows, maybe the new world you wish to see will come to life, sooner than you had thought.

Richard Tyler

Therapist, Coach, Best Selling Author of Jolt: Shake Up Your Thinking and Upgrade Your Impact for Extraordinary Success

Richard is here to disrupt the coaching industry. As we drown in gurus who promise the world, but fail to deliver, Richard offers a fresh and creative lens to encourage you to look within.

Richard works with executive leaders to help them navigate these unchartered territories we find ourselves in.

"Can I Have a Word?"
Management Training Session

Introduction

How many times do we hear the phrase, *"Can I have a word?"* in the workplace, at home, or at the organisations where we are members?

What emotions does this little phrase evoke? Whenever I have heard it in the past it screamed: *"Oh no, what have I done now?"* Am I the only one?

After many years as a Management and Leadership Trainer and Coach, working at great depth with the whole concept of dealing with performance, attitude and behaviour in the workplace, I have seen time and time again the problems attached to *"Having a word"*.

I am writing this book to help people deal with those difficult, often traumatic and sometimes explosive discussions in a more positive way for everyone involved. In my career as a Transport Manager, a National Sales Manager, a Director in the Civil Service, and Training Manager within tour operations and the airline industry, I have witnessed first hand how conversations fail to go the way they are planned, how control is quickly lost, how swiftly the blame

Can I Have A Word?

Can I Have a Word? Manager's Perspective

Can I Have a Word? Staff Member's Reality

for something turns back on the Manager and how Managers start to flounder.

I have watched people lose control of the conversation, take offence, become defensive, or watched many mangers tread warily around the subject without getting to the real point.

What is even worse is when there is no plan of action after a conversation – what was the point of that?

I have experienced first hand a very stressful disciplinary and *"Chat"* situation in my management career. It's painful. So I needed to search out a remedy!! This book HAS the remedy.

The renowned principles of *Dale Carnegie* in his book *'How to Win Friends and Influence People'* will permeate through this book. I was an Instructor with the *Dale Carnegie Organisation* for 16 years, it is amazing how many of Carnegie's principles still apply today when dealing effectively and constructively with other people.

In fact one of Carnegie's principles is, *'The only way to get the best of an argument is to avoid it'. (*Principle 10 in *How to Win Friends and Influence People.)*

I do not want you to avoid the conversation, just use better skills to stop it becoming an *'argument'*.

During my years as a Leadership and Management Trainer I have discovered the

MAGICAL WORDS which turn negative or conflict situations into positive and forward-moving situations for both parties.

Simple techniques win every time

I have developed six simple techniques to steer Managers through the emotion and difficulty of *"having that word"*. The important element is *'SIMPLE'*. My training style has always been to create simple techniques which people can put into immediate use in the workplace and recall them easily time after time.

The six techniques I will share with you will intertwine. They will rarely be single operations. I see it a bit like a recipe. The basic recipe stays the same and you make different dishes by merging some new ingredients. I have built up these techniques with corresponding pictures, so you can link the pictures to the methods.

I found out very recently that I am dyslexic and have dyscalculia (number dyslexia). I always wondered why, in my training I created simple methods and diagrams to explain ideas and systems to people. That makes sense now.

So, I have written this book to make it easier for all to read. I have included illustrations and video links to enhance learning and make the techniques and messages memorable.

The videos show how the six techniques work in practice. They run alongside the book to add more depth and help you see the impact subtle changes in words can make on the overall result. The book provides the reasoning behind the techniques, the videos depict the development. Both will make it easy to read, learn, watch and reinforce.

The videos can be viewed after each section by scanning the QR codes in *Resources and References* or go to www.suetonks.com and follow the links.

The book and videos accompany you through simple methods of keeping control, finding solutions, creating stronger relationships, monitoring results positively without appearing to do so openly.

These simple techniques will enable you to get the best from yourself, your team and create success and harmony in the workplace.

They will help you deal effectively and easily with those difficult conversations we need to have with people from time to time about all aspects of behaviour, attitude, and performance.

Learn the magical sequence of words to move you from an inevitable and sometimes explosive argument, to a calmer understanding, a valuable and worthwhile conversation and, even more importantly, an agreement to change.

But it can't stop there! Having those **MAGICAL WORDS** with someone is no good if we fail to adopt the correct method of following it up.

Many managers have said to me,

"Sue, I don't feel right following up after I have had to talk to someone, as they might see it as bullying or picking on them."
I totally understand.

But what if there was a way that you could follow up on the changes you agreed the person would make without appearing to be monitoring openly?

In the following chapters will be able to identify:

- What emotions are evoked then we need to *"Have a word"*?

- Which words work.

- Which words can spiral downwards into major conflict.

- How easily Managers can lose control of the discussion.

- What causes the control to switch when dealing with a touchy situation.

- How you can help create a positive plan of action.

- How you can ensure progress is maintained without monitoring openly.

- How excellent performance, attitude and behaviour can be achieved and maintained and reinforced.

I will help you:

- 🏃 Have those conversations.
- 🏃 Stay in control.
- 🏃 Create a positive outcome for everyone.
- 🏃 Allow you to follow up and ensure the person is continuing on the right track.

How does that sound?

But why limit this advice to business, or school and sport settings? Never a week went by when I heard, *"Susan, I want a word with you,"* at home, when I was growing up. So, this advice can also help when dealing with a variety of situations at home with the youngsters, partners, in-laws, and neighbours. In-fact any setting where you need someone's attitude, behaviour or performance to alter or improve.

This book is highly practical and has specific case studies bring the techniques and problems to life to make sure you don't fall into the same trap.

The videos will allow you to see these **MAGICAL WORDS** happening in glorious technicolour. You will be able to identify situations, jot down approaches and plan to follow these simple techniques yourself.

Please use this as a workbook. Prepare yourself with a pen or pencil and watch the videos at the strategic points to see for yourself how these magical words and techniques work.

Some of the techniques join with others, like the recipe I mentioned earlier, so it will create a bit of an equation: This + this = this. So, you can relate to the techniques in a pictorial style. Get me, using equations!

When you have read this book and put the techniques into practice, please feel free to leave a review and let me know how it helped!

Ready to start? Let's go.

Chapter 1
The Effect on Others

What happens when we hear, *"Can I have a word?"*

Well, if you are anything like me, I feel a strange sense of doom and foreboding – even if I haven't done anything wrong! When we hear it, we automatically fear the worst, look at what we could have done wrong, start to justify ourselves and our actions, and search for what we might say or do in our defence.

I heard *"Susan, come here, I want a word with you!"* from my mum and dad at all stages in my life (note the Sunday name when they were angry or annoyed with me).

I remember when I was about 10 years old, sitting in the classroom when the Headmaster walked in pointed to me and said, *"Tonks...a word!"* Not even *"Can I...?"*

I followed him out of the room; fear and dread gripped me as he moved through the school quickly with me tottering and trembling behind. He motioned me to sit down on the chair outside his office to wait.

Terrified

I waited, the fear built up, I felt sick, I wanted to cry. I was sure I was going to be expelled... but why? What had I done?

Who would put a child through this?

A few long agonising minutes later he called me into his office, he said, *"Tonks, we have been watching your attitude and behaviour"* (now that was it, I was definitely being expelled) *"and we have been delighted by the way you have conducted yourself this year, we would like you to become a Prefect."*

Well, who would have thought it? I believed I was in for the chop and look at that – he floored me with the total opposite. You never can tell with *"Can I have a word?"*.

In a recent survey, I asked people to describe to me the feeling those five little words evoke. The response was very interesting, not just the feeling and emotion they evoked but the consequences of those five little words.

Let's have a look at what emotions and feelings were evoked first.

92% of my survey respondents talked about the same feeling of foreboding I have always experienced.

Sally said, *"I can't say it's happened often, but it is a phrase I tend to view in a negative way... I get a flippy tummy and an overwhelming feeling of dread that I've done something wrong... either someone's complained about me, or I've* *said something inappropriate... the list goes on...! It induces a physical response of heightened anxiety, with sweaty palms, racing heart and rapid heart rate... classic fight or flight response. When it has been said to me it generally hasn't been a bad thing, so the natural response I get is unwarranted but nevertheless it's deeply unpleasant!"*

Jess told me, *"What on earth have I done wrong (again). Belly churning, argument provoking and a negative outcome is the only outcome. I feel undermined, inadequate, worthless, all my feelings are negative ones."*

Baz said, *"It was mainly negative in my experience – One of your team is not towing the company line and needs to be addressed was a common 'Can I have a word?' discussion. Then I would have to convert those words into something positive to my team member to bring him or her up to scratch by encouragement, but I never said to him or her "Can I have a word". I praised them in public to encourage them to believe in themselves."*

This can happen from a senior person, or on the other hand, as many of my responders showed, it can be upwards from a staff member to their Manager or Supervisor. The effect is often the same. Here are a couple of examples:

Dan said, *"Interestingly the time it was said to me was by one of my employees who wasn't happy because her holiday request had not been sanctioned because someone else was already off at the same time. By starting the conversation with "Can I have a word?" she put my back up straight away so I it was probably a less than sympathetic conversation."*

Karen commented, *"In my previous business as a lingerie shop owner we employed eight staff. Staffing was the hardest part of the business and we constantly felt totally reliant on the rotas etc. If someone left or called in sick it sent everything into chaos. So, when anyone said, 'Can I have a word?' it filled me with fear and panic!"*

Alternatively, these five little words can be said by a person wanting a bit of help or support. This can throw you off balance, as you can see here:

Mo said, *"I agree, on occasion it can be that you are in trouble, or about to be given bad news, but I have also found it is often said when someone is asking for advice or asking for an opinion and sometimes seeking reassurance."*

Sandra commented, *"A staff member asked if they could have a word. I immediately felt that sense of dread in* *the pit of my stomach. What had I done wrong? In fact, they simply wanted to explore whether they could switch their working from home day to another day as the washing machine repair man was due!"*

Alastair, with 25 years of experience as a Line Manager, now business adviser, mentor and coach said, *"People have asked 'Can I have a word?' many times over the 25+ years I've been in line management roles. It has caused all sorts of emotions. It was the opener from one lady who had had a significant period of absence for mental health reasons, but I'd thought she was doing well three months after returning. She wasn't struggling again - she was pregnant. Relief. About three months later another female member of my team said it. She had gone from a temporary to permanent position twelve months earlier, when we had made her permanent. She told me (unprompted) she and her partner had given up trying to have a family. Guess what? the stability of a permanent job had helped reduce the stress from the process, and it worked. It is scary to think both those kids are now teenagers!"*

Sarah said, *"In 1993 when I was about to emigrate to New Zealand, one of my colleagues in the investment bank where I was working said 'Can I have a word in private?' He was about to take over from me as the head of the department when I left. I said 'Of course,' and we found a quiet cafe. Over a glass of wine, he told me he was gay and he felt he needed to keep this a secret at work - but felt he wanted to tell me as a friend. I think he felt safe telling me as I was leaving the company. I felt honoured he could share this with me."*

Sometimes the news you were dreading comes at you at full speed, as Billy and Wendy told me,

Billy said, *"I was sitting at my desk finishing up my eulogy for a very close friend who died from cancer of the brain. The funeral was the following day. My mobile phone rang. I didn't recognise the number. A male voice introduced himself as a Consultant Urologist. 'Have you time for a chat? Can I have a word?' His voice was quite quiet and pleasant however this was a call* which *had come out of the blue. I recalled having my bloods checked for Prostate-Specific Antigen levels a few weeks before however wasn't sure when I was going to be notified of the results.*

7

I expected to receive a letter, not a phone call. As I thought this through my anxiety levels increased and I expected the worst. He then went on to tell me I had been diagnosed with prostate cancer. Foolishly, caught up in the emotion of the moment, I let him know what I was doing at the time of his call. He was immediately apologetic however went into some detail of the low-grade prostate cancer I had and what the options were. 'Can I have a word?' historically, for me, is the foreword to not good news!"

Just to let you know Billy is well and spends much of his time raising money to help villages in Rwanda. He and his wife, Fiona, take regular visits to Rwanda to carry on their great work.

Wendy had a similar experience, *"I heard those words said by my boss's boss. My boss was on holiday in the US and his boss was camped out in his office with the HR Director. I knew straight away this either meant a restructure or me out of the door. After a couple of minutes of what they felt was 'setting the scene' it was the latter! If I ever hear those words again, I will always link them with bad news!"*

Billy is no stranger to this phrase and presented me with another story,

"Can I have a word?" was said to me the day after my boss was laid off when I

worked as a Unit Financial Controller at an in-flight catering company at a local airport. The words came from a chap (who had a smile on his face) who I had met very briefly the day before when he first came to the premises. As I was in charge of all the sensitive areas of the job, including the preparation of monthly accounts, costings of menus for all of the airlines and negotiating costs with suppliers, I assumed I was going to be promoted. Little did I think in less than an hour later I would be getting escorted off the premises with staff accompanying me to my office to make sure I didn't access any of the highly classified information which would have been gold to our competitors. I wasn't even permitted to say goodbye to my staff or the other staff members. A lot can be hid behind a smile."

When I was the Training Manager to a major Airline and Tour operator I had a new boss. He came with me to a meeting where I had applied for a substantial grant funding for NVQ qualifications for our Overseas Representatives. Having sat in on an extremely positive and lucrative meeting, he told me he had been really impressed with how I handled it. He said I knew all the answers to the questions, had worked out the finances perfectly and had gained the funding required. I was delighted.

To have my new boss witness this and be so positive about our project and the results which was incredible.

Then he said, *"How about we go for coffee, I would like to have a word?"*

When we sat down at a local hotel for the coffee he launched in and said, *"I am going to give you two choices, either take a demotion or go down a disciplinary route – and be sure I will have you out."*

I asked what I was supposed to have done and he said, *"I don't think you are communicating with your team."*

I was totally stunned. I didn't have a team. I only had a part time assistant, who sat next to me. How could I not communicate?

He told me to take the rest of the day off to think over my options and tell him first thing the next morning. Wow! Where did that come from?

You just never know, do you?

I loved this job and certainly did not want to go down a disciplinary route. His vehemence frightened me, and I knew he would carry out his threats, so I chose the demotion in the hope I could resolve the situation.

I later found out I was not the problem. The Director was having an affair with my Assistant, and it was pure vengeance for something which had happened to the Assistant in another role.

The Director also did not like the fact I was not interested in him! Not long after I was demoted the Director was arrested on a variety of charges and later imprisoned.

Sadly, the Company did not right the wrongs, and regardless of the fact it was the best job I had ever had, I decided to leave. What a waste.

Isn't it amazing how many emotions these five little words have: positive, negative, fear-inducing and in some cases relief? What is even more amazing is the long term and profound effect these encounters have on us and our lives.

How do Managers Feel?

As a Manager, or Supervisor preparing for the *"Can I have a word?"* discussion can be equally as traumatic. Most Managers work out their justification for having **"THAT WORD"** several times.

They start practicing WHAT they are going to say and HOW to say it. Going over and over it.

Managers can and often put off having **"THAT WORD"** in the hope things will improve, they hope the subject will comes up naturally, or as if by **MAGIC** the problem will disappear like a puff of smoke into the ether!

Delaying the conversation may make the Manager feel better - in the short term - and many times they *don't* want to make a scene, they *don't* want to ruin a good working

Good and Bad Gollum

relationship, they ***don't*** want to demotivate the person or the team, they ***don't*** want to create upset. They ***don't*** want to be NOT liked.

How many more DON'Ts do we need?

This avoidance mechanism reminds me of a little character I use in both my Networking Training and Time Management training. It's *Gollum* from the J R R Tolkein's book and film *The Lord of the Rings* and *The Hobbit.*

Gollum stars in three books and six films. Throughout these books and films there are two sides to Gollum: Gollum and Sméagol – good Gollum and bad Gollum.

Good Gollum says, "Yes, we needz to sort out the problemz, findz a solutionz, stopz problemz from happeningz again. We likesezz dealing with problemz and gettingz resultz. Bezt dealz with it quickly in the beztest way!"

Bad Gollum then chips in, "Ahh no! We dontz likeeez confrontationz, what if they get angry, what if they shoutz back, what if they not happyz with me? No... we don't likeeez dealing with problemz. We likeezz ironing or googling insteadz! We likeeez keeping friendzzz!"

The internal battle continues.

AVOIDING THE ISSUE MIGHT SEEM A SHORT-TERM FIX but it rarely deals with problems long term.

This book will allow you to understand your reticence in approaching the person and problem, plan effectively and make sure you have tools to deal with the situation in a speedy way without causing upset, long term problems or worsening relationships.

Chapter 2
The Human Response

What could possibly be worse than these five little words, **"Can I have a Word?"**

If we thought the human emotions of those five words were bad enough, Managers and Supervisors can make it worse creating even more difficulties. How?

By telling us **WHY** they want a word.

This is when the person tells you a tiny bit about, *"What you have done"*. For example: *"Can I have a quick word about your project/ your customer/ your letter/ your sale/ your bedroom."*

There it is! The cat's out of the bag and the staff member starts to justify themselves and create a defence even before the manager has moved into the next sentence.

This gives the person time to get their hackles up, prepare a defence and starts the conversation on a **defensive-attack mode**. How could you possibly be in both defence and attack at the same time? - That's easy.

The thing with a defensive mode is it quickly turns to attack, and oh boy does it explode!!

KEY POINT: Never say: "Can I have a word?" and never tell them WHY you want a word.

What could you say instead?

There are a lot of suggestions from my survey:

- 🏃 "Have you got time for a quick chat?"

- 🏃 "Time for a coffee?"

- 🏃 "Have you got a minute?"

- 🏃 Or even - easier to say: "Have you a second?"

These are less confrontational, and leave it at that, a second gives the impression of something quick and easy. Bingo! This is what we want.

Natural Fight or Flight Behaviour

As human beings we are programmed to operate in a specific way when we are faced with conflict or danger. This is called, *'fight or flight'*.

We either automatically gather all our energy to fight, using our widened body language, making us look bigger and more menacing, like a cat which arches its back, and its tail stands tall. All our energy and power condense into this fighting action.

17

Or we put all our energy into our legs to run away and get us out of the situation as quickly as possible. There have been many illustrations over the years of the enormous strength, power, and energy we can create in perilous situations to get ourselves out of danger or help a loved one in peril, such as lifting cars and fallen buildings, running for miles on difficult terrain.

Let's have a closer look at the natural behaviour of someone who suddenly feels accused, even if they haven't done anything wrong.

These days we rarely need to go into full flight or fight mode, so what we do is **internalise** the danger. This can harm us even more as human beings in today's society, as the inner turmoil starts to materialise as stress. This causes many internal difficulties which affects our central nervous system, creating panic attacks, ulcers, high blood pressure and behaviour changes. This is due to the normal flight or fight mode feeling paralysed - so something has to change inside us if our strength and energy is not being externally transmitted.

You might think this only exists for the team member but no, it also exists for the Manager as both are in a stressful situation.

People's responses are to either:

  🏃 Turn the situation into a joke and be light-hearted about the meeting, while they start to create a defence for their actions in their mind. Or,

🏃 They start to get really worried and nervous which disables their thinking and speaking processes.

Once in this frantic panic, the fundamental and natural responses are flight – avoid the situation (not attend the meeting, go off sick, etc) or fight, and be prepared for battle.

The Joke Response

The Joke Response reminds me of the silly things people say when questioned by a police officer, or customs official. You know, silly remarks like, *"It's OK officer, there is nothing in there except only my dead granny's cat"* or *"I only have a pile of bullets and booze behind there"*. As a Magistrate for 22 years, I have heard lots of comments people have made to Police in jest, as a way to get themselves out of a tricky situation or just the fear of a strange situation. Never a good tack to go down, believe me!

When I was Training Manager for Airtours, the comments we heard from people who were nervous or worried - especially at check-in or customs - were mind boggling, *"You won't find a bomb in this suitcase as it's in the other one"* or, *"I packed my gun in the bag – be careful!"*

These sorts of comments would lead to the person being taken away by security and on many situations, their bags were retrieved, and they were sent home.

Teflon Man or Woman

The Fight Response

When people feel they are to be attacked they make it a personal attack, which naturally kicks off our fight or flight mode. This can be unsettling for us and can dramatically alter our behaviour.

The fight response is generated automatically to protect themselves. They put up barriers and shield themselves usually, in situations where they can't run away. They achieve this by blaming everyone else, the situation, the weather etc. They put their shield up and start shooting from behind it.

I call it Teflon Man or Teflon Woman.

Teflon Man is the nickname given to John Gotti because he was charged with different crimes multiple times but he was never convicted as the charges would never stick, hence the name Non-Stick.

The Teflon Man/Woman is an expert at outlining why:

⚹ Nothing is ever his/her fault.

⚹ There is always a well quantified response and excuse of why an action plan failed.

There is always something out of his/her control when a target has not been achieved, such as:

⚹ The environment.

⚹ The people.

21

- The product.
- The scarcity of resources or support.
- The timing.
- The market conditions.
- Anyone or anything - but it will never be about him/her.

Physical Responses to Fight or Flight

Regardless of the verbal response there are usually physical changes when someone feels threatened: tightness of muscles, particularly in the shoulders and arms; sweaty palms; the fear of impending doom in the stomach; dry mouth and the  cold shivery feeling creeping up the back and up the neck where your hairs stand on end. Recognise it?

So, with all this emotion going on it's hardly surprising so many discussions, no matter how well intended, can turn in different directions, creating totally unexpected situations.

As a Manager we need to be aware that this naturally happens, and the physical feelings people get are natural too. Many people cry when approached with a difficult situation. Why do we cry?

Dutch psychologist, Ad Vignerhoets in 'Why Only Humans Weep': Unravelling the Mysteries of Tears says, "Crying

22

is primarily a form of nonverbal social communication aimed at eliciting assistance, comfort, and social support from others. Research to date has shown when people see others crying, they clearly recognize it as a reliable signal of sadness or distress (in a way it's more convincing than words) and it typically results in feelings of connectedness and responses of sympathy and a willingness to help from others.

So, it's often a **CRY** for help, support, or love. Now we are aware of the changes which start to happen in a person before we *"Have a word"* it will help us better prepare for those difficult conversations.

Identifying How your Team Members are Performing

Many years ago, when I attended my first Dale Carnegie Management Seminar, which was a six-session management development programme. I was introduced to a simple method of categorising members of my team so that I could understand where they were in terms of performance levels and what they brought to the team. This method allowed me to create a development plan for each of them. This method quickly allowed me to determine where the team were in terms of performance, behaviour, attitude and skill and what I needed to do with each of them to move them forward.

It was a simple ABC method. Its simplicity and total practicality enabled me later, to create my own management techniques, which were also simple to learn and to apply, including the techniques in this book.

This method uses ABC twice. This is how it goes;

Think about each of your team members and give each of them an A B or C in the CURRENT role they are doing.

A= The person is performing their job to the level and standard required in their current role.

B= the person has the potential to perform to the level and standard required in the current role but are not there yet.

C= The person does not have the ability to perform to the level or standard required in the current role.

Next, think about each of these team members in a HIGHER ROLE or given HIGHER LEVEL RESPONSIBILITY. Again, allocate an A B or C.

A= They are ready now for a higher role or higher responsibility.

B= They have the potential for a higher role or higher responsibility but are not there yet.

C= They do not have the ability for a higher role or higher responsibility.

This will give you six categories: AA, AB, AC, BB, BC, CC.

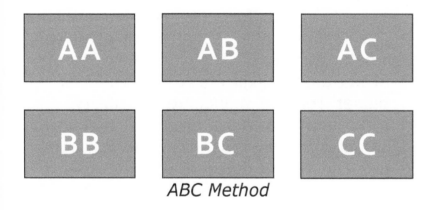

ABC Method

With these categories you can then start to establish where the person is and where you need to take them to be totally effective in your team, department or organisation. For example, if you have an;

AA They are already performing to a high level consistently, they have all the job knowledge and skills in the role, they are providing quality performance and take little supervision time. However, they are ready now for a higher role, so need a development conversation to grow them ready for a higher role, or they may become stale and bored and subsequently leave. When a manager delegates to them it needs to be a whole responsibility not just petty tasks.

AB You have someone who is really good at their job, consistent, and performing their job to a great standard. They are not quite ready for a higher role, so their development plan would be to establish what specifically they need in terms of knowledge skill etc to be ready for a higher role or higher responsibility. In their enthusiasm to progress they can sometimes overstep the boundaries so the manager would delegate smaller tasks to them and monitor projects more carefully.

AC This person performs at a consistent level. They know their job inside out. They need minimum daily supervision. They are the rock on which departments are built. They provide the stability in the team. But if you had too many of them in a team there would be no creativity, growth or change. ACs do not necessarily like change. They are happy doing their job, day in day out. They are also settled and regardless how good they are at their job they may not want or seek promotion.

However sometimes you may get an AC who believes they are an AA and not only capable of a higher level but READY now. This has its own challenges for a Manager. Sometimes the conversations they have to have, are around behaviour and attitude, rather than knowledge or skill.

BB If you have a BB in your team, the first thing a manager has to focus on is moving the first B to an A, as until they are an A they are not performing to the level required for the job. This BB may be new to work, new to the job, or new to a section of that job. They may be an enthusiastic learner. However, they may also have ALL the skills required to do the job but are not performing to the level required. This leads to a difficult, but necessary, conversation.

BC This person may also be new to the role or task, but even if you change the B to an A they will still be limited because of the second C. On the other hand this could be normally and A who is not performing in his or her job at the moment and slipped from an AC to a BC.

Any person can slip down in their performance, even an AA, depending on the situation. Generally, this is related to an attitude or behaviour issue within the team or person.

Which of course needs the "Can I Have A Word?" conversation.

CC The CC is a strange one, usually this is due to poor recruitment, inheriting people from other departments, or the job technical skills have out-grown the person's ability.

However, sometimes this is only a temporary situation if the person is usually an AA, AB, AC, or BB. Something else is going on behind the scenes, maybe even outside the working environment, for the person to be performing to this standard.

Again, this is one of those times when you may need to "Have A Word"

With each category, once you have established what needs to be done to get the best from that staff member you can prepare the conversation.

If there is a gap to fill, for example a BB to an AB, or an BC to an AC you can start to address this gap. You need to establish whether the gap is knowledge, skills, attitude, performance, or behaviour, or a mixture of any of these.

Sometimes it requires a straightforward training plan and building in time for experience. Sometimes, however there might be need to "Have A Word" to put the person on the right track or 'back' on the right track.

I tell you this as later in the book we will be looking at four case studies, and it will be useful to identify what is required to help the staff member perform to the level required to do an excellent job.

In case study one we will meet Vivi (short for Vivienne) she is an AB who is struggling with managing a project. This is holding her back. This could be related to her skills in project management but could also be linked to her behaviour or attitude. You will find out.

In case study two, we meet Vivi again this time she is normally an AA, but something has slipped and she is currently a BB. What needs to change and how? As a Manager or Supervisor you would need to deal with that.

In case study three we meet Victor; Victor is currently a BC bordering on a CC. He is causing major problems in the job and for the rest of the team. By looking at what Victor needs to do to improve you can start to formulate what needs to be addressed and the results you need. When you meet Victor, you will realise the complexities of the situation.

Finally, in case study four we meet Vivi again. This Vivi should be an AC but currently her attitude and behaviour and performance moves her more towards a BC not an AC. However, this situation is made more difficult as Vivi believes she is an AA (with delusions of grandeur). She thinks she is not only performing brilliantly but is overdue a promotion. Sounds tricky!

When a Manager understands how his/her people are performing and knows where each team member needs to be in terms of knowledge, skills, attitude, performance and behaviour, the Manager can work more effectively with each team member to achieve top- level performance.

When Managers need to have those 'conversations' the techniques in this book will help them to achieve these results.

Look Forward Not Back

Chapter 3
Technique 1 -
Look Forward Not Back

The Start of the Conversation

In this chapter I will introduce you to the first of the six techniques I have developed over my many years working in Leadership and Management Training and Development.

The first technique is called, ***"LOOK FORWARD NOT BACK."***

We know people will be more highly strung, defensive, weepy, argumentative, confrontational (the list is endless) when we address a delicate or tricky situation. As Managers and Supervisors, we need to be ultra-careful of the situation we may create and remain in control of the discussion throughout.

But is it this easy? I wouldn't be writing this book if it was. I am never surprised by the speed of the shift of control from Manager to employee, from good friend to enemy or doting

Meet the Cast of the Videos

parent to the "worst dad or mum" in the world.

No matter how many times I talk to Managers about how they are going to approach the "difficult conversation" - EVERY Manager I talk to makes the same fatal error. When I say EVERY Manager - I mean EVERY Manager. I will explain what this fatal error is shortly.

In case study 1 below, you will meet a character called Vivi (short for Vivienne), she appears as different staff members throughout the book along with Victor.

My Dad always wanted me to be called Vivienne but when I was born my mum found out it was the name of one of his earlier girlfriends...so I became Susan (which is my Sunday name, or when my mum is in a bad mood with me).

Case Study 1

Please read the following case study and write down how you think you would start this **_"Can I have a word?"_** conversation with Vivi. Here's how it goes:

CASE STUDY 1 - Manager's Viewpoint

Vivi has been with the company for 19 months. She learned the job quickly.

She has very good rapport with customers, and you hoped you could use this strength on an important project for the department.

Recently Vivi has been given a project to start up and lead. Not only was it important for external relationships but required a lot of internal cooperation.

However, this project did not meet deadlines, resulting in panic with Vivi and the team working flat out in the last two days of the project. Many mistakes were highlighted in the project when completed, and the main purpose of the project was not met properly.

Due to other considerations the company had been forced to change the focus of the project from the one initially expressed.

Vivi's future prospects looked good for promotion, but she has now been held back by this recent problem.

Vivi is keen to progress and is bored with the present job, hence the giving of the project in the first place.

As Vivi's Manager:

- 🏃 How would you prepare for the discussion you are now about to have with her?

- 🏃 How will you start?

- 🏃 What will you say?

Vivi is an 'AB'.

Please write, in detail, what you would say.

Now you have written your thoughts, let's look at the two ways most Managers start in this scenario.

Regardless of how long you thought about how you would tackle this case study, and how much experience you have had in dealing with such discussions, I have realised Managers and Supervisors hit several pitfalls in the road in what seems at the outset, a pretty straightforward route.

What could be easier than *"having that word"* when you have thought it through, and probably practiced it a few times beforehand?

How were **YOU** going to start the conversation? I would like to introduce you to two pitfalls:

"The Path of Impending Doom" and,

"The Deep Pit of What Happened?"

1) The Path of Impending Doom

The Path of Impending Doom is the route taken by many Managers who have been told in their previous management training to "avoid conflict", "start on a friendly note", and create a nice "chatty start"... the advice goes on and on.

This technique often fails to work.

"IMPENDING DOOM" is a wandering path, meandering along with little twists and turns, ambling along quite gently, but going nowhere.

This is the technique Managers use to avoid broaching the problem situation in the hope the staff member may say something which allows the contentious issue to be brought up WITHOUT THEM HAVING TO DO IT THEMSELVES.

It goes like this...

Manager: *"Hi Vivi how are you, great to see you, how's the Squash going...?"* Pause...

"I hear you won last night?" (Pause)

"How's the job going?" (Pause)

"I hear you had a new customer on a call yesterday?" (Pause)

"How are relations with Z section going, I hear you had a few challenges?..."

It is during this process, which seems to drag on and on, when Vivi starts to feel uneasy. She is not sure whether to say the job is going great or not, or that the relations with Z section are absolutely fine *or not*. It's a dilemma for her!

Vivi is unsure where this line of questioning is going and searches for some other signals from her Manager, while trying to assess the situation.

Impending Doom

However, she is faced only with smiles and a neutral, if not over friendly tone, from her Manager – she can't read the situation and is unsure how to respond.

Her dilemma is, does she say everything is fine and brush it off, or admit there were problems with the project? **NO** she doesn't want to do that.

So, she just responds in a non-committal way, saying as little as possible... awaiting an opportunity to get away physically and emotionally from the situation, and hoping her Manager will give something away so she can see just which path he is taking her on.

This reminds me so much of the effect the *'Dementors'* – one of the characters in the *Harry Potter* books.

For anyone who has seen those films or read the books the Dementors *"suck the life out of you"*. They conjure the icy-cold chill feeling of total despair and hopelessness which creeps slowly through the victim.

You might think this is a bit dramatic... but when you have been there and witnessed it for yourself – it isn't dramatic enough!

39

The Effects of Impending Doom

The effect of the Manager avoiding the issue usually results in the staff member feeling the hairs on the back of their neck stand up, an eerie chill creeping through their body. They feel on edge and the feeling of IMPENDING DOOM slithers slowly upward. An icy cold feeling takes over. They have a growing sick feeling in their stomach, their mouth gets dry, and their chest tightens. NOT a pleasant experience.

Now the staff member is getting worried, their mind races forwards, desperately trying to find the right protection and armour for this strange form of attack.

Dale Carnegie says, *'Begin in a friendly way'* (Principle 13 in *How to Win Friends and Influence People*).

Whichever way you start please START. Staff do not know where this line of questioning is leading, and total anxiety takes over. Here's how it sounds:

Response from Vivi

Manager: *"Hi Vivi, how are you? It's great to see you."*

Vivi: *"Yes good thanks"*

Manager: *"How's the squash going, I hear you won last night?"*

Vivi: *"Yes it was a great match, a struggle right to the end but I dug in deep..."*

Manager: *"How's the job going?"*

Vivi: *"Yes, good thanks..."*

Manager: *"I hear you had a new customer on a call yesterday..."*

Vivi: *"Yes, it was a lead from the one of the guys in department Z – got great potential..."*

Manager: *"How are relations with Z section going, I hear you had a few challenges?"*

Vivi: *"Great thanks, they are a nice bunch."*

Sound familiar? In this approach the Manager is trying to get the staff member to move the discussion into the *'problem'* situation by his/herself, and to let the Manager off the hook.

But with Vivi's response the Manager realises the plan is NOT working. This causes the Manager a bit of anguish as they hoped it would all pop out in the wash, and they wouldn't have to BRING THE PROBLEM ISSUE UP at all.

The Managers IDEAL response from Vivi 2:

If Vivi says, *"Oh, the job has been a bit hard recently during the project..."* then **bingo**, the project *"issue"* has been brought up and the Manager doesn't need to broach it with him/her first. Saved! Phew.

Vivi isn't really likely to go down this line, and make the Manager's job easier. No – not a chance.

Many people (Managers included) hate confrontation and use this *"around about the houses"* method to try to get to the point, without ever getting to the point. It leaves the poor Vivis of this world struggling to work out whether the Manager is being interested, kind or is **ready to pounce**.

You might think, *"Well that sounds okay, I get it... so I will get straight to the point and avoid the painful route of Impending Doom..."* only for you to land feet first into: **"The Deep Pit of What Happened?"**

2) "The Deep Pit of What Happened?"

What I am going to describe to you now is **THE** major pitfall Managers land themselves in when they actually start a discussion about someone's performance, behaviour or attitude.

When I run this session in my Leadership and Management Programmes, 93% of Managers start the same way and hit the same hurdles, then wonder what went wrong!

Only 6% use the Impending Doom approach – never getting to the crux of the matter - and the remaining 1% can't start at all!

Once you understand this simple pitfall, you will realise how easily you have lost control before and suddenly been turned into the "bad guy" without warning.

Here is the worst starting comment you can use as a Manager... (but 93% of Managers start like this):

Manager: *"Hi Vivi, great to see you, please sit down...*

You won the squash match last night, brilliant, it was tough opposition I hear.

As you know Vivi I gave you a project to lead, which I knew you had the skills to deliver, but as you know the project was subject to many problems and was late missing its deadline. What happened? or What went wrong?"

Now you might think, "Hey OK, that's a nice polite start, and the Manager commented on something Vivi did - the squash game, then asked the question directly about the project failure. No prevaricating – good job done."

Well, no, ***"What Went Wrong? or What Happened?"*** is the worst thing you can ever start with. You have landed with total immersion into *'The Deep Pit of What Happened?'*

43

In Video 1 you will see this exact scenario unravel in front of your eyes. You will see why the Manager lost control of the situation and how Vivi took control of the meeting. The Manager was suddenly put on the back foot and struggled. (To view this video go to Resources and References and scan the QR Code for Video 1 or *view the video in* www.suetonks.com).

Believe me, this ALWAYS happens. Why?

Earlier I explained what happens physically, emotionally and mentally when people feel threatened. They go into fight or flight mode.

Well, the *"What happened?"* or *"What went wrong?"* type of start immediately evokes the fight mode. Their shield goes up to protect themselves and they start shooting back from behind the shield to any available target... usually the Manager!

Remember Teflon Man/Woman, where nothing is ever their fault? It is at this exact point when the excuses come in, the person shields themselves and the blame blasts out in all directions.

These defensive explanations are normally always prefaced by:

- 🎵 I did my part, but they didn't do theirs...

- 🎵 The problem already existed even before I got here...

🏃 There's only so much I can do if the team is demotivated...

🏃 I can't do much when the people I work with lacks the skill...

🏃 I could have made this successful if I would have had the support...I could have achieved the target if we had started earlier...

🏃 It is a struggle to perform because the environment and the product is just too complex...

And so much more variations and permutations of the same thing: "It is not my fault".

"What happened?" or "What went wrong?" is the worst question you can ever ask.

If you only take away one golden nugget from the whole of this book, let this be THE golden nugget!

The One-Sided Viewpoint

One of the difficulties for Managers addressing performance, behaviour or attitude issues is they often see things only from their own viewpoint.

Rarely what the Manager sees and experiences is the same for the individual. So, let's have a look at the scenario and experience again, from Vivi's viewpoint.

45

CASE STUDY 1 - Vivi's Viewpoint

Vivi likes the job very much but is getting bored and wants to progress quickly. She has been in the current role for 19 months.

She has been frustrated with the project recently given by her Manager. She was expected to achieve major results for the department by heading up a team of people from different departments. The project would benefit the customer.

Problems with the project arose as Vivi was not sufficiently briefed by the Manager. Information she required was not easy to come by, and other departments failed to produce information on time to meet her deadline. Vivi had a few arguments with other departments due to their lack of cooperation, even her own team had not been committed to help despite needing to take part.

Vivi found out, quite late on that the Management changed the goalposts, from what they initially expected from the project.

Vivi is very upset with the situation, however, feels inside she didn't organise herself and others as much as she could have done (but won't admit it openly).

Hold on to Your Hat

Knowing this, we can now go back to the *"What Happened?"* question posed by Vivi's Manager and experience the result.

Manager: *"The project you did for me Vivi, as you know didn't go quite as planned, what happened?"*

Vivi: *"What happened! I'll tell you what happened...*

Firstly, I didn't think I was briefed effectively in the first place. (Vivi's voice increases in volume!)

You didn't let the other departments know what information and help they were supposed to give me.

I wasn't given the time to do the project and when I came to you with problems on the project you were always too busy to discuss it with me.

Then I found out you had changed the goalposts right at the end.

THAT'S WHAT HAPPENED!"

Wow!

- 🏃 Who's in control now?

- 🏃 Where is the blame of this project failure sitting with now? and,

- 🏃 With who?

Asking *"what went wrong?"* or *"what happened?"* is the biggest mistake we can make.

The staff member quickly turns the tables, everything is everyone else's fault and, more often than not, the blame shifts directly on to the Manager. The staff member gains control, and the Manager then starts to defend him/herself.

One-nil to Vivi.

Now the Manager is in the pit, scrambling to get out.

I hope you understood just what happened here. Now I am going to send a ladder down the deep pit of "What happened?" to help you climb back out.

Technique 1: Look Forward Not Back

When something has gone wrong, don't start by asking "What happened" or "What went wrong". This will only cause the person to be defensive and shift blame out to everyone. They will put their shield up, hide behind it and shoot out in all directions.

The problem has already happened, you can't change it, but what you **CAN DO** is ensure it doesn't happen again.

Looking back at the problem causes the most pain in these situations. But 93% of Managers fall into this trap!!

Believe me, this is so easy to fix.

All you need to do as the Manager is to focus **ON THE FUTURE.**

 As the future situation has not happened yet, the staff member does not need to get defensive, or worried. They become more open and, as a result more progress gets made.

Also, there is no need for conflict as neither party is talking about a real situation – but something in the future. Something which has not existed yet.

Let's show you how this works. In Vivi's case, the Manager would say:

Manager: *"As you know Vivi I gave you a project to do recently – which was well within your skill set. Unfortunately, as you know, it didn't go according to plan. If I gave you a similar project to do in the future, what would you do differently?"*

Wow, what a difference this makes. Instead of Vivi hiding behind her shield and shooting out to everyone - mainly her Manager - Vivi could reflect on what she would do differently or what needs to happen differently next time.

Here are the important words, **"Next time"**. So, her attention is not on self-protection but looking forward. Here is what Vivi could say:

> **Vivi:** *"Well firstly I think I would need a better briefing at the start, to ensure the full objectives were clear.*
>
> *I think the other teams could be informed about such projects earlier in the process and what they could do to assist me."*

Sounds good so far.

Sometimes though, people stop after two or three points which may not be enough of a change required to fix the full extent of the problem. So, here we will introduce the second technique: ***"What else?"***

51

Chapter 4
Technique 2 - What Else?

The little phrase *"What else?"* releases the floodgates on suggestion and ideas to avoid the same problem happening in the future.

Here is how the situation continues...

Manager: *"Great idea Vivi, what else could you do differently next time?"*

Vivi: *"Maybe we would need more regular reviews and catch-up sessions together. This would help as often you were too busy to see me."*

"What else?" or *"What else would you do?"* This is a great way of asking for more information. You will get one suggestion after another and as these occur, write each one down.

So you don't sound like a broken record it is important to add some extra words occasionally rather than just "What else... what else...?" all the time. This helps to break the cycle and refocus the person on what you are asking.

You could use something like:

"What else would you do in a situation like this *again in the future?"*

"Great idea, what else would you do next time?"

It is important to ensure you have all the solutions – so it may take a few *"What elses?"* before you have reached the desired result for the future.

Each time you say: "What else?" or its longer equivalent, PAUSE and wait for the answer.

I know pauses might seem difficult. We are programmed not to like pauses and feel we need to interject to break the silence. They make us uncomfortable.

But it is important to wait for the answer.

Sometimes if the pause is very long just repeat the question, *"So Vivi, what else would you do in the future?"* and wait again.

The big temptation is to answer the question for her. **Don't!**

Think of the process as a chart going from the starting point – which is what happened - to achieving the future goal.

Then think of moving towards the end result, goal or target behaviour with every suggestion the person gives you.

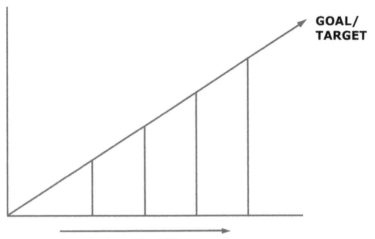

EACH "What else?"Suggestion

Sometimes the staff member may give you four or five suggestions. Regardless how good or bad these suggestions are – WRITE THEM DOWN. Never discuss, argue, or give them your own ideas.

In this case if I was Vivi's Manager I would be writing:

- Better briefing at the start with full and clear objectives.

- Brief other teams on information required about such and what they need do to assist you.

- Regular talks to other departments so they stayed on track with the information you might need.

- Involve your own team more, rather than take up all the work yourself.

Remember this is the staff members ideas and suggestions NOT yours.

Imagine you have the chart (shown) – each suggestion the staff member gives you moves another section towards success.

When you have asked "What else?" and the staff member cannot think of another, and you have been patient and waited, but there is definitely nothing coming back... This is your chance to **"TOP UP"**. We TOP UP with our own suggestions to bridge the gap."

This is what it would look like on a chart with each line getting you close to the target performance, attitude or behaviour you would like to see.

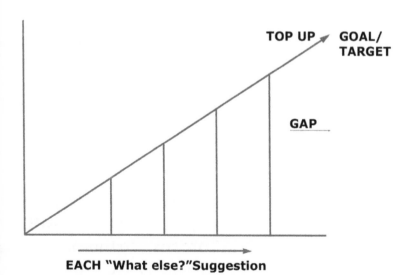

EACH "What else?"Suggestion

TOP UP

After the staff member has made several suggestions but they are not quite getting to the result you desire, you may see there is a gap between the level of performance, attitude or behaviour you would like to see and their suggestions.

It is at this point, and this point only, you TOP UP with your own suggestions to achieve the final result.

This is the last resort, though. **DO NOT TOP UP** until all other suggestions have been made.

If the staff member makes all the suggestions themselves and they meet the required level of performance, you are looking for, then the **TOP UP** is not necessary.

Recap the Suggestions

Before you **TOP UP** you need to **RECAP** what the staff member has already said. This is because the Manager wants his/her idea to be attached to Vivi's suggestions. The point of this is that, if all Vivi's suggestions go first the additional suggestions from the Manager join onto them.

In my leadership and management training I use a communication process called **SARI** (**Seek, Act, React** and **Inform**). In this process the technique we would use is **ACT BUILD**. This means building on someone's ideas with your own. This takes their idea and adds yours onto it to add additional strength to their action and gets your ideas cemented into theirs. In this way it feels like it is their own idea, and they accept it more readily.

SARI is a technique I use to show managers and leaders what words and sentences are greater influencers than others when we are trying to get our point across in meetings, negotiations, conferences etc.

This is what TOP UP would sound like with Vivi:

Manager: *"So Vivi what you said you would do next time is ...*

Make sure you had a thorough understanding of the brief before you started.

You said you would want me to brief any other teams to ensure they were aware of your project work with them.

You said you would talk to the other departments more regularly so they stayed on track with the information you might need.

And you said you would involve your own team more, rather than take up all the work yourself. How does that sound?"

Vivi: *"Yes that sounds about right"*

(and now for the TOP UP)

Manager: *"And how about you schedule in regular sessions with me at the start to review the project's progress, initially one a week to get it started and later perhaps every other week, so if there are any difficulties they can be dealt with in a timely fashion? How does that sound?"*

Vivi: *"Yes that's great, thank you."*

'Hey Presto', you have fitted the final piece into jigsaw, the solution for the next project to work successfully.

Let's have a look at this section again, and highlight some magical moments to help you in the future:

- Firstly, we got all the suggestions out first by asking "What else would you do (in the future)?"

- Secondly, we wrote each suggestion down as they were said (we never argued or contradicted).

- Thirdly, we repeated all the suggestions to the person and asked: "How does that sound?" We waited for a response from the person.

- Fourthly, if there was a gap between the person's suggestions and a future successful performance, we repeated all their suggestions and then TOPPED UP with our own.

🏃 Fifthly, we asked again: "How does that sound?" and we got a response from the person/staff member.

If all this goes to plan, then put the staff member back into the future by saying:

Manager: *"Well, Vivi if there is a project for you to do in the future, I am sure you will tackle it with great success by taking these actions."*

You will see above I used the words, *"How does that sound?"* I could have used; *"How does that feel?"* in my explanation above. But you can use different words depending upon the staff members learning and communication style – if you know it.

Later, I will explain why using different types of words for individual staff members, family members etc is useful if you want them to take on board the information you give them.

Look Forward Not Back

I have been working with this *"LOOK FORWARD NOT BACK"* technique for many years and was delighted to see it starting to appear in many performance review meetings.

My friend, Richard Tyler in his book, *Jolt*, talks about changing the word *'feedback'* to *'feedforward'*.

For those of you who are eagle eyed, Richard has written the Foreword. He appropriately says:

> *"Feedingforward - offering suggestions and insights for how to move forward, by making positive changes to THINKING, SKILLS, and ACTION."*

He goes on to say:

> *"It is far more useful to help people learn to be 'right' than to prove they were 'wrong'. This can become such a waste of energy and yet it is what happens much of the time with the giving of feedback.*
>
> *Whereas feedback can become slow and lumbering, drawing attention to faults and mistakes, feedforward can be delivered with some pace and energy."*

Richard also mentions:

> *"The term feedback in an organisation brings a strong gut reaction, an emotional flooding of the body. Feedback can be associated with criticism and judgement."*

This sounds exactly like the emotions we experience when we hear, *"Can I have a word?"* or *"What happened?"*

Thank you Richard!

It's all about emotion and response, fight or flight or protection.

Chapter 5
Finding Solutions

One of the big mistakes Managers make is coming up with solutions to fix the problem in the future themselves, rather than letting the staff member identify their own solutions.

Why is this important? Well, it is so easy for Managers to tell the team member what they should do in the future, or what they should have done. Managers may well have more experience, and know many of the answers but their suggestions rarely create BUY IN from the staff member.

It is important that the team member finds their OWN solutions. If you, as the Manager/ Supervisor offer your suggestions such as more training, better project organisation, identifying a project plan etc the person will go into a *"Oh yes"* mode. You might be familiar with this character... the *"nodding dog"*.

This is how it goes:

Manager: *"So Vivi next time make sure you have a clear idea of the brief at the start and make sure everyone who is*

Ohh Yes

involved is briefed and communicate regularly... how does that sound?"

Vivi: *"Oh yes."* (Nod)

Manager: *"And how about you attend some training on project management to help you with the organisation – how does that sound?"*

Vivi: *"Oh Yes."* (Nod)

The person goes into Nodding Dog mode and says, *"Ohh yes, Ohhh yes, Ohhhh yes".*

If the solutions come from the Manager the staff member will pay lip service to them. They won't **OWN** them.

If the problem reoccurs the person can separate themselves from the actions and say, *"Well it was your idea, it was your suggestion not mine."* And bang! The blame goes back to the Manager.

If the Manager comes up with all the solutions to the problem they become *"Mr Fix It".*

Dale Carnegie says; *"Let the person feel the idea is his or hers"* (Principle 16 in How to win Friends and Influence People).

William C Byham and Jeff Cox in their book, *Zapp!* says, *"Provide support without removing responsibility for action".*

MR FIX IT tells the staff member all the fixes for the problem they faced.

Although the Manager may well know all the

Mr Fix It

fixes, it is more important that the person identifies their own.

Managers can easily take over the discussions and show the staff member all the things they should do in the future.

Why do they do this?

- 🏃 Firstly, they are keen for a speedy way to finish the discussion and get out of the tricky situation.

- 🏃 Secondly, it allows them to get CONTROL of the conversation back.

- 🏃 Thirdly, it can show how CLEVER they are.

The solutions should come from the staff member themselves and they OWN them.

Get All Solutions First

The flow of a conversation is very important. When the staff member is on a flow of possible solutions the last thing the Manager wants to do is stop that flow.

That's why we introduced the term, ***"What else?"***

List the solutions, do not discuss them. Remember we mentioned that in the last chapter.

It is vitally important to get **ALL** the solutions out into the open and avoid fixing any of the solutions there and then.

If you discuss every **FIX** as it is mentioned, you will start to go off on a tangent, the meeting will not flow and you will loose the impetus for more ideas. It will stop the team member focusing on their future fixes.

One of the areas where Managers lose this momentum is around *"the idea of training."*

Here is how it goes:

Vivi *"I think I could benefit from more project management training."*

Manager: *"Great idea Vivi, do you want to go on an external training course, or would being mentored by one of the other Managers be better for you?*

Would you like a computer based training programme on a modular basis or a one off training programme?"

This *"butting-in"* stops the continuity of conversation which can quite easily get side-tracked into totally different conversations and directions.

Leave the discussion about each suggestion until all ideas have been offered. Better still, discuss the solutions at a later meeting, giving both parties time to think.

As long as we both have clear solutions and agree on them the rest can happen later.

After you have discussed the fixes then run through these actions again – the action plan. Finally get commitment by asking "How does that sound?" or "How does that feel?"

We will discuss how to end the meeting later.

Let's have a recap at this point.

RECAP
1. Know the target performance.
2. Get actions to bridge that gap.
3. Top Up to fill the gap.
4. Run through the actions again.
5. Get commitment.
6. Close the meeting.

C.R.

Chapter 6:
Discovering the Real Reason

You might be saying at this point: *"Hey, hold on we haven't discussed with Vivi about what really happened to the project, why it failed, why other departments were upset, why it missed its deadlines. Aren't we missing something?"*

Quite right, we haven't. We don't need to. We already know. Vivi has already told us what happened, and she didn't even realise it.

So, let's have a look again at why we have just gone through this process.

- Don't ask: *"What happened?"*

- Look to the future instead (If you were to be in this situation again, what would you do differently?).

- Listen and write down every suggestion, asking: *"What else?"* until you are happy the next time it will be successful.

- Don't stop the flow or the suggestions.

- Repeat the suggestions, asking: *"How does that sound?"*

71

🏃 Top up with your own additional answer last if necessary,

🏃 Recap and ask: *"How does that sound/ look/ seem?"*

Why we ask the future question is to get to the REAL reason why the problem of performance, behaviour or attitude happened in the first place.

The responses Vivi gave in Case Study 1 in the previous chapter are NOT excuses or blame - they are in fact the real reason the project/ behaviour/ attitude/ performance failed in the first place.

When we ask: "What happened?" or "What went wrong?" we get excuses and blame as they hide behind the shield and shoot. This is non-stick **Teflon Man/Woman** again.

When a person is talking about something happening in the future - it doesn't cause any difficulties. It is not a threatening place; they can address future project difficulties and most importantly the Manager stays in control.

When we ask a FUTURE question, *"If you were to be in this situation again, what would you do differently?"*, we get the real reason why it occurred, without the blame, shielding, power loss etc and certainly much less of the attitude.

It's amazing... so much so, I should write a book on it!

So, have we finished with this first example? NO. These are still a few lessons we can learn. The first is identifying WHO is to take the action in the future.

At this point the Manager may be thinking:

A. These answers would ensure future projects would work sufficiently.

B. These solutions would go a long way to ensuring other project succeed, but there is a bit to go yet – so there is a need to top up.

C. Vivi has not taken personal responsibility for the failure of this project.

If the Manager thinks (A) these answers would ensure future projects would work sufficiently, then next step would be to repeat these points.

Manager: *"So, Vivi if I was to give you a project like this again you said you would want to make sure you were fully briefed beforehand and understood the brief before you started. You would want all departments to be fully briefed about their participation beforehand. And you would make sure all people involved in the project were communicated with throughout the project term. How does that sound?"*

Vivi: *"Yes, that sounds fair enough."*

Manager: *"OK so let's take these plans forward when the situation arises again."*

If the Manager thinks (B) these solutions would go a long way to ensuring success in future projects **but** there is still a bit to go yet to get optimum performance.

Then the Manager would make a slight amendment to the above statement:

Manager: *"So Vivi if I was to give you a project like this again you said you would want to make sure you were fully briefed beforehand and understood the brief before you started. You would want all departments to be fully briefed about their participation beforehand. And you would make sure all people involved in the project were communicated with throughout the project term. How does that sound?*

How about we plan in advance at least one meeting every two weeks to make sure the project stays on track, and I am there with any help you need to progress it further? How does that sound?"

Vivi: *"Yes, that great."*

This is the **TOP UP.**

If the Manager thinks (C) Vivi has not taken personal responsibility for the failure of this project, then a simple addition to the scenario is required.

How would we know? Well, it's simple – if Vivi failed to say the word, 'I'.

Taking Responsibility for the Outcome

You can always tell if people do not take personal responsibility for a project, task or situation. They assign actions to everyone else and take no responsibility themselves.

Here's how it sounds in Vivi's scenario – you have seen this before but may not have noticed.

Manager: *"Hi Vivi, please take a seat. It was great to hear you won the company squash tournament last night, good going. I heard it was a hard match, but you dug deep. Well done. Vivi, you know the project you led for me, I understand there were some difficulties with the information you needed from different departments, and it failed to meet its deadline. If you were to do a similar project in the future – what would you do differently?"* (LOOK FORWARD NOT BACK)

Vivi: *"Well firstly you need to brief me fully on the goals and expectations.*

The Managers of other departments should be briefed, they need to make sure the information is available.

Can I Have A Word?

Taking Responsibility

You would need to be more available during the project.

The teams would need to work to their project plans, and you wouldn't change the goal posts without discussing it?"

Here you can see, ALL the action points in the future are the Managers' and other team members - NOT Vivi's.

Vivi is not coming up with any solutions which affect her – she is managing to get all the responsibility for future actions and corrections passed onto others.

If you are getting the words, "They, you others..." etc and the staff member is not saying "I" then they are not taking responsibility.

How do we fix this? It is simple: at the end of the discussion before summarising add the final sentence – "If this situation happened again in the future what would you do personally differently next time"

The person would have to answer with the word "I".

Here is how it goes.

Manager: *"Vivi these suggestions are great, and will certainly help future projects succeed. What would you do PERSONALLY differently next time you did a project like this?"*

The Manager then shuts up and waits.

Vivi: *"Well... I suppose I would organise myself differently"*

Manager: *"In what way, Vivi?"*

Vivi: *"Well... to do a better plan and remember to ask the team and the other departments for information in advance rather than expecting it from them straight away."*

Well, there we have it: one of the main reasons Vivi's project failed! Phew!

Vivi told us, she didn't manage some of it as well as she could have done.

When Vivi used the word, 'I' she was in fact taking personal responsibility for some of the problem herself, rather than it being everyone else's fault. We also saw a glimpse of what caused the upset between Vivi and the other departments. This aspect didn't come out before. Vivi has no alternative than to answer, *"Well, I would..."*

When we have this personal admittance that not everything was other people's fault, we get to the REAL crux of the problem.

Vivi did mention her planning of the project wasn't as good as she could have done. There may be a training need here in the future. But let's leave this aside while the going is good, we can always come back to her later with an idea of future training.

Now we know what **actually happened** with Vivi's project.

I told you it would all come out. No one got upset or lost control. So, let's just finish the conversation for now.

Finishing Off the Conversation

As explained earlier the Manager would go back to his/her notes and say,

> **Manager:** *"OK Vivi, we know the project didn't go according to plan, but if I was to give you a project again you would...*
>
> *...and you also said you would organise yourself better next time by managing the project planning better and communication to the team and other departments earlier to get information you need. Is that right?"*

> **Vivi:** *"Yes that's right"*

> **Manager:** *"Well OK Vivi if I give you a project again in the future you have a plan of how you need to tackle it next time. How does that sound?*

> **Vivi:** *"Yes that sounds fair."*

> **Manager:** *"Great then, let's see how it goes. Oh, and Vivi thank you for taking on that customer enquiry the other day. It was a difficult one and you tackled it well."*

Vivi leaves the room with the last bit of praise ringing in her ear and... a plan for the future.

We were fortunate Vivi was quite happy with what was said and the future solutions. If the conversation doesn't go as well (that's if you didn't follow my advice), the outcome can be very different.

Infecting Others

Chapter 6: Discovering the Real Reason

Infecting Others

Many times, when someone has been taken into an office *"to have a word"* they can come out of the office, feeling badly done to, upset, aggrieved etc, and the first thing they do is start infecting others around them with negativity.

> *"Oh I can't believe that! Guess what they just said to me?"*

And they sound off to other team members saying things like; not my fault, unfair, picking on me again etc.

The staff member tries to get support from others and creates bad feeling in the department.

They succeed if they can bring others around to their negativity. In James Redfield's book, *The Celestine Prophecy*, he talks about the *'Poor Mes'*. These people - like the *Dementors* in *Harry Potter* I mentioned earlier - gain energy and power by sucking the life and energy out of the other person.

I have met many *'Poor Mes'* in my life: neighbours, colleagues at work, customers. The similarity between them is: they moan about everything, nothing is right, and they always have a worse deal than anyone else in the world. Even if you say, *"Good morning"* to them, they respond with, *"What's good about it, if you would have had the night I had you wouldn't say good morning."*

Filming Vivi for the Video

You can't win with a *'Poor Me'*, their whole objective is to bring you down and take the energy from you.

When someone doesn't feel they have had a fair hearing - their entire mission is to infect everyone else with their negativity, to suck other people into their situation and onto their side.

So how do we stop this and fix it forever?

Finish with Praise

Again, like all the techniques and ideas in this book, it's simple. Here is how it goes...

> **Manager:** *"Well OK Vivi, if I give you a project again in the future you have a plan of how you need to tackle it next time. How does that sound?"* (LOOK FORWARD NOT BACK)
>
> **Vivi:** *"Yes that sounds fair."*
>
> **Manager:** *"Great then, let's see how it goes. Oh, and Vivi thank you for taking on that customer enquiry the other day. It was a difficult one and you really tackled it well. The Customer contacted us to say he was really pleased with the result. Well done."*

Dale Carnegie says, *'Make the other person happy about doing the thing you suggest.'* (Principle 25 in *How to win Friends and Influence People*).

You may have heard of the *"Praise Sandwich"*, which I call a ***"HAPPY BURGER"***. It has been a technique used by Managers for many years. This is why we start feedback with praise and end feedback with praise.

We will come back to this in a different case study. There is a lot to the ***HAPPY BURGER*** Technique so best left for later - but it's worth mentioning briefly at this point.

By taking the ***HAPPY BURGER*** route this is what happens:

Happy Burger

Manager: *"Great then, let's see how it goes. Oh, and Vivi thank you for taking on that customer enquiry the other day. It was a difficult one and you tackled it really well. The Customer contacted us to say he was really pleased with the result. Well done."*

Vivi will feel she:

- Has been told off to a certain extent.
- Has an agreed a plan of action.
- Knows what she will do in future situations to make it successful.
- Knows not everything she does is negative.
- Has been openly recognised for the good work she has done.

So now, when she walks back into the office, she stays quiet, and doesn't infect others. Even when asked, *"How did it go?"* by a colleague she would shrug and say, *"Yes it's all fine"* then smile and get on with her job.

Phew! Problem averted.

The final part of this section is about making sure people do not feel they are taking on the full burden of finding and acting on the solution alone – even if they are.

We can achieve this by ***offering a helping hand***.

Offer a Helping Hand

Offer a Helping Hand

The staff member, family member, or whoever you are *"having a word"* with must never feel that the problem and solutions are theirs alone (even if it is). It is important to share a bit of the responsibility with them.

I call it *"offering a helping hand"*.

Always look at the solution of a problem as a joint effort. Use words like, 'we' , *"help"*, and *"together"*.

So, in Vivi's case her Manager might say,

Manager: *"Well, Vivi what can we do to make sure this sort of thing doesn't happen again in a future project?"* (LOOK FORWARD NOT BACK)

Note the word 'we', "What can we do?"

If we use the word **'You'** ("What can YOU do to make sure it doesn't happen again in the future?). It sounds a little harsh but saying 'we' makes all the difference.

It shows the actions and solutions are a joint effort and certainly softens the sentence.

Vivi: (might answer) *"Well, you could brief the other teams earlier, and perhaps have regular meetings with me."*

What if it Happens Again?

The *'me'* shares the actions and responsibilities. If Vivi also brings in an *'I'* and says,

> **Vivi:** *"...and I would work on organising what I needed from the teams in advance",*
> it strengthens her commitment to make changes herself.

Remember, if Vivi was ONLY giving you the responsibility without taking any herself – (if the *'I'* is missing) you would need to then say *"OK, what would you do PERSONALLY next time?"*

So, is this all? Are there any more nuggets to discover?

Well, yes. In this case study there is ONE more thing to uncover.

What If It Happens Again?

What if you gave Vivi another project in the future and it failed?

How would you start your conversation with Vivi this time, knowing what you have learned so far? Write your answer in "Your Thoughts" on the opposite page. Do not move on until you have given this some thought.

What If It Happens Again?

Many Managers smile when I ask them to do this as they think, *"Ah this is easy, I learned last time never to ask what happened and to look at the problem in the future."*

So, they start with: *"As you know Vivi I gave you another project, but sadly, as you know it didn't quite according to plan. If I was to give you a similar project in the future – what would you do differently?"*

This sounds OK, doesn't it? **But no!**

How many chances are you going to give a person?

What happens next time: are you going repeat the process yet again?

You discussed and agreed what Vivi needed to do the first time – she had a PLAN of ACTION, but it didn't work again Argh!

How do we fix it?

Here is the punch line...

...*"WHAT HAPPENED?"*

This time you **CAN** say, *"Well Vivi, this second project you have undertaken... what happened?"* and leave it at that.

Vivi will have no excuses, she will not be able to shift the blame to anyone and she will have to accept it went wrong.

In Video 1 you will see this exact situation occurring. You will see the total resignation on Vivi's face. She has no words, she can't defend herself so admits defeat, quietly and contritely.

Wow, what a transformation.

What the Manager can do, at a later time, is to work on what further training and development she may need in the future, if he/she were ever to give her a project again.

RECAP

Don't ask "What happened?"

Look to the future instead.

(If you were to be in this situation again, what would you do differently?)

C.R.

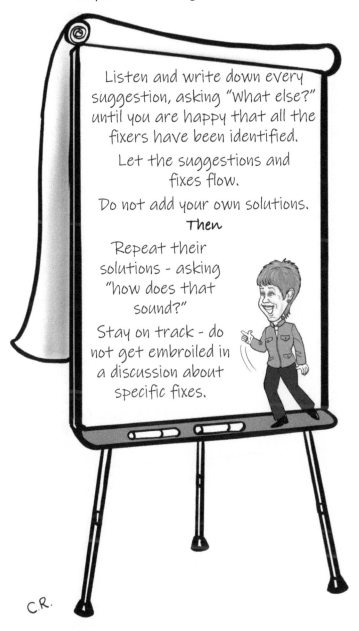

Listen and write down every suggestion, asking "What else?" until you are happy that all the fixers have been identified.

Let the suggestions and fixes flow.

Do not add your own solutions.

Then

Repeat their solutions - asking "how does that sound?"

Stay on track - do not get embroiled in a discussion about specific fixes.

C.R.

To watch the video, go to Resources and References and scan the QR Code. Or go to www.suetonks.com and follow the link.

Top Up with additional suggestions last if necessary.

Offer a helping hand.

Make sure the person has taken personal responsibility for some of the actions - with an 'I'.

Ask **"what would you do personally next time."**

Then

Recap the solutions again and ask **"How does that sound/look/seem?"**

Finish on a good note by praising some aspect of their performance.

C.R.

Chapter 7
Technique 3 - Focus Technique

As Managers we need to focus our attention on the performance, behaviour and attitudes of our team members. We need to look at how their actions link to productivity, customer relations, internal activities, and the company as a whole.

Many staff need to liaise externally with clients, suppliers, and internally with other teams. They will be constantly interacting with people on different levels in their roles, face to face, remotely, over the phone or internet. Over the last two years much of our interaction with Managers, colleagues, customers and suppliers has been over Zoom® or Microsoft Teams®. There are many situations where problems may arise.

Where you have identified a difficulty with a staff member relating to performance, attitude or behaviour you may consider using a different technique to **"LOOK FORWARD NOT BACK"** to start the process.

This is the **'FOCUS TECHNIQUE.'**

Before I explain, please look at the second case study and once again decide how, as Vivi's Manager, you would tackle this situation

Write notes at the end of the case study, then we will explore the options again.

Zoom Lens Camera - FOCUS TECHNIQUE

CASE STUDY 2 - Manager's Viewpoint

Vivi has been with the Company for eight years, six of those in this department. She has applied for promotion several times, but has never been successful, although she is extremely knowledgeable and skilful in the current role.

Recently her attitude has been quite sharp with customers, and several complaints have been brought to your attention.

Vivi has become bitter towards others in the team, particularly to the two younger members she was mentoring.

She has also recently upset other members of the team and is currently unusually lacking enthusiasm.

Vivi's product knowledge and the practical elements of the job cannot be faulted.

She recently wrote a training programme for new starters into the department which went down really well.

> She would normally be considered to be really good at her job and has the potential to progress to the next level but her recent behaviour worries you.

How would you deal with this situation when you call Vivi in to "Have a word"? Vivi is an 'AA' but slipping down to a 'BB'. Write your answers below:

FOCUS TECHNIQUE

Imagine a Camera with a ZOOM lens. You start off the image on a wide angle, then ZOOM into the specific part of the picture you want to focus on.

Below are pictures I took of a Bulrush at a lake near my house. In the first picture we have a wider view of the scene. In the second picture I have zoomed into a specific area to see the image in much closer detail.

This is exactly the technique you can use to deal with performance behaviour or attitude.

Wide Angle

Zoom In

How did you do with Vivi's second Case Study? You may have started the same way as you learned with the first scenario with the "LOOK FORWARD NOT BACK" technique. That's fine.

However, let's identify a second technique of dealing with the *"Can I have a word?"* discussion.

This is called the FOCUS TECHNIQUE.

Here is how this would go:

Manager: (WIDE ANGLE) *"Hi Vivi, firstly can I say, I was really impressed with the Customer Service training module you wrote the other week, your knowledge of the systems and processes in this department are second to none. Which is*

CUSTOMER SERVICE CALL CENTRE

Great Customer Service

why I wanted to talk to you further.

Usually, you have a fabulous relationship not only with the customers but also across the team. I have always been impressed with the way you have handled customers -particularly difficult ones.

(ZOOM IN) However, over the last few weeks I have been sad to hear there have been some complaints from customers about your attitude – particularly Mr Evans from Dodge and Co. who said you shouted at him when he complained a delivery had not occurred on time.

Also, I overheard you being really short in your response and attitude to Sash and Yvonne, your mentees, when they have asked questions. They are both new and

CUSTOMER SERVICE CALL CENTRE

Poor Customer Service

of course they don't know everything yet, which is why you are supposed to help them.

Yvonne got quite upset and I heard she cried in the ladies toilet afterwards.

This is not like you Vivi. What can we do to make sure this kind of thing doesn't happen again in the future?"

Then listen and wait.

You will realise at this point we have now re-joined the technique "**LOOK** 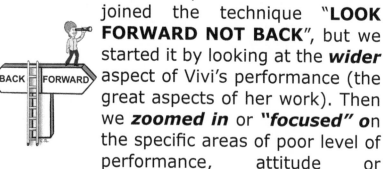 **FORWARD NOT BACK**", but we started it by looking at the *wider* aspect of Vivi's performance (the great aspects of her work). Then we *zoomed in* or *"focused" o*n the specific areas of poor level of performance, attitude or behaviour which is currently appearing.

There are a few reasons why I suggest this. Most people have good if not great aspects of their work. Very few people are poor at everything. By looking at the good behaviour, performance or attitude the person usually portrays, then "focusing" in on the specific areas causing a problem, it helps to show the person that not all is poor, and you accept they are normally very good at aspects of their work.

Remember this issue with performance, attitude or behaviour might be just a temporary

102

situation. You certainly hope so. So, to "nip it in the bud" early enough might make life easier for everyone and maybe the matter will not get worse.

Many Managers and Supervisors fail to deal with problems soon enough: they think it may be a one-off and won't happen again. They may be scared of appearing too harsh, or worse still, bullying. We discussed this delaying tactic at the start of the book, remember, with Gollum?

It is vitally important for you to deal with issues before they get worse, get out of hand or progress to a higher level.

You will also notice another element in the Managers discussion with Vivi – the '**SPECIFIC EVIDENCE'** the Manager highlighted.

This is another key aspect of the FOCUS TECHNIQUE but can be integrated into the other techniques quite easily.

Specific Evidence

For 22 years I have had the pleasure of being a Magistrate. I was the Chairman of the Bench, which meant I sat in the middle of two other Magistrates in the Magistrates' Court. Our job was to hear evidence on criminal cases, and on the basis of that evidence, we had to judge if a person was guilty or innocent of a criminal offence.

Get Evidence

As a Magistrate, we had to rely fully on the evidence given and make our judgement on that evidence alone.

If the evidence was not presented to us, we couldn't make a judgement on it. I have to tell you it was frustrating at times, as we couldn't ask questions to flush out some missing evidence. If it didn't come out in the case, we couldn't consider it in our deliberations.

The same applies to evidence we have relating to a person about an incident, behaviour, attitude or performance issue.

If, as a Manager, in Vivi's case you were to say, *"Vivi I have heard you have had a few difficulties with customers you have had arguments with them, and recently you have been short tempered with colleagues."*

Then Vivi would be right to defend herself and say, *"What customers have I had complaints from? You tell me which colleagues I have upset and when?"*

She could be defensive and throw it back to the Manager to come up with specific evidence. If you don't know the specific information you will be on the losing side and look foolish.

105

If you are aware of specific situations, actions etc, then you must mention these. It is important to be specific not woolly or wishy-washy when addressing issues of performance, attitude and behaviour.

If you talk about specific situations, people, behaviours etc, then the person will have less of a cause to argue with you. It will be easier to get onto, "What can you do in the future?" route.

The following comments are not specific enough to pin down or deal specifically with behaviours or performance:

- *"Sometimes you are a bit curt and short with people."*

- *"You have been late for work a few times recently."*

- *"You have often failed to reach the deadline."*

If you fail to be specific the person can hit back. And they will! Unless you can back up your findings, you will find yourself on the back foot and struggling to be taken seriously.

This is how the Vivi might respond:

Manager: *"You are sometimes a bit curt and short with people..."*

Vivi: *"What do you mean curt, which particular person or customer, when* *exactly, what exactly am I supposed to have done?"*

Manager: *You have been late for work a few times recently...*

Vivi: *"Which days and by how much, I suppose you are not looking at the times I have actually been early and ready for work before others have even arrived?"*

Manager: *"You have often failed to reach our call target..."*

Vivi: *"Which targets, the ones you changed without telling me, the ones when I was covering for three people who were off sick?"*

Instead, you need to provide specific evidence:

- "Yesterday I overheard you being really sharp with a customer when they were saying their goods had arrived faulty, you raised your voice and interrupted them several times."

- "You have been late for work on five occasions over the last month, two of these times you were more than an hour late, and three times you have been 10 or 15 minutes late."

- "Twice in the last month you have not hit your call rate deadline; the first time you were just 4% off target but the second time it was over 11%."

107

What makes good EVIDENCE?

Well just like any objectives we can use the SMART objective measure for our evidence. This stands for:

Specific – not woolly or wishy-washy.

Measurable – anything which is measurable will have a £, number, date or %. If it has two of these it will be more measurable.

Achievable – it can be achieved within the parameters of operation.

Realistic – given the time frame, situation etc.

Timescale – this is usually a date or time frame. e.g. from 1 April 2022 to 30 March 2023; by 1600 on 18th May 2022; starting from 1 June 2023 onwards.

Hearsay

Another problem we may face as a Manager is dealing with a situation we have heard about from someone else.

In Court, as Magistrates, we always had to watch out for HEARSAY. This is when someone gives evidence about what someone else said or did e.g. A witness testifies: *"Susan told me Tom was in town."*

Unless Susan was also a witness in court this statement would be known as hearsay, and not accepted as evidence.

How does this affect you as a Manager or Supervisor?

Many times, we may hear of a problem or difficulty from another person. It could be another staff member, another Manager, or even a customer.

Did this specific action or incident happen TO THEM? Or are they relaying the information from what they have heard.

If it happened to them, then this is direct information or evidence, but if they are telling you about something someone else has said then this is hearsay which needs to be investigated further.

You need to be very careful with this; establish the specific evidence, and not take the other person at their word.

There may be specific reasons for the team members' behaviour, attitude or performance which the other person was not aware of or, worse still, the other person might have a vested interest in telling you about it, or have a grudge to bear. Just like the experience I talked about earlier with my Manager and my Assistant where she had a grudge and fabricated information to get her own way.

It is always important to investigate in order to have the facts before addressing the situation. Knowledge gives you power, gets your message across clearly and you keep in control.

If you are receiving information from other people, it is always best to thank them for their information and say you will look into it in greater depth. Then you can investigate further - even if the information is coming from someone more senior. We don't know how or where they are getting their information from.

Balance the Evidence

Can you remember the evidence about lateness earlier?

> **Manager:** *"You have been late for work on five occasions over the last month, two of these times you were more than an hour late, and three times you have been 10-15 minutes late."*

You have been specific, given a number and a time period, so, besides the specific dates (which you could have with you) you have all the evidence you need.

But still, it might not be all plain sailing, as you do not know the reasoning behind the actions (or lack of them) and the person's situation.

So, it is important to hear from them too. You cannot think evidence on its own is good enough. The information needs to be balanced. Let's see how the conversation with Vivi might go.

> **Manager:** *"You have been late for work on five occasions over the last month, two of these you were more than an hour late,*

and three times you have been 10/15 minutes late."

Vivi: *"Yes the 10/15 minutes was when I had to go to Reception to pick up the 'signed for' - mail before starting my shift, and there was a queue at Reception with visitors arriving.*

One of the days it was my turn to pick up the mail, the other two days I did because other colleagues were either ill or on holiday.

One of the two longer periods of lateness were due to my child minder getting delayed. I phoned in and spoke to the Duty Manager straight away to let them know I would be late.

The other time I hadn't been well in the morning but came in anyway, but it took me longer to get here, and I am sorry"

Well, where do you go from here? Maybe the fact you have brought the matter up will be enough to put future lateness in check. Or maybe you can apologise as you were not fully aware of the circumstances. Certainly, this doesn't sound like ongoing poor behaviour or attitude from Vivi.

Sometimes when we hear the person's response it sways our thoughts and actions.

This is what evidence is for.

It would be a sad state of affairs in a Court of Law if we only heard the Prosecution's side of the argument. So, it is important to balance the information before you act.

Contrary Evidence

Sometimes you may look, not to how many times a person has been late, but how many times they have come in early, worked late, or done additional shifts.

It is always important to look at performance, behaviour and attitude in the round. Look for contrary evidence, especially if the information you have been given is from a third party... the information might be skewed!!

Zoom back out to the wide angle

When you have addressed the performance attitude and behaviour you need to zoom back out to the wide picture again.

This is vitally important, as you need to show what the results of the change in performance, attitude or behaviour will achieve for the person, wider team or the company. This closes the loop. Here is how this might go with Vivi

Manager: *"So, Vivi if   you   ... and you ... you will find that it ... How does that sound?"*

Always ask for the person's response at the end.

This is what the FOCUS TECHNIQUE looks like as a picture.

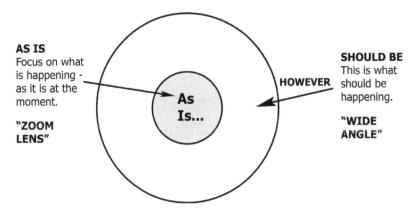

Focus Technique

We start off the process by focusing on the wide angle – What the role, job task SHOULD BE like. Then we zoom or focus into the "AS IS" (as it is at the moment), with the word HOWEVER.

We deal with the fixes using the "What else?" method we have used before, and when we are all happy the solution has been achieved, we zoom back out to the bigger picture (wide angle). Just like you would with a camera.

Wide ⟶ Zoom ⟶ Fix ⟶ Wide

The Term, 'However'

HOWEVER is an important word, many Managers use BUT.

Using the word **BUT** creates negativity. It adds a confrontational edge to the sentence. 'HOWEVER' softens the sentence.

You will have heard this in conversation many times:

- "I don't mean to be nosey, but..."
- "I don't want you to take this the wrong way but..."
- "I'm not being funny but..."
- "I don't want you offend you but"

It always means the opposite.

Here is the conversation with Vivi

Manager: *"Usually, you have a fabulous relationship not only with the customers but also across the team. I have always been impressed with the way you have handled customers - particularly difficult ones. BUT over the last few weeks I have been sad to see there have been some complaints."*

Or

Manager: *"Usually, you have a fabulous relationship not only with the customers but also across the team. I have always been impressed with the way you have handled customers - particularly difficult ones. HOWEVER over the last few weeks I have been sad to see there have been some complaints."*

114

HOWEVER makes it far more palatable and less confrontational. Heavens above, it's hard enough having these conversations without causing even more bad feeling!

VAK Learning Styles

This is a great time to introduce you to the importance of specific words for different communication and learning styles. This way we can use the best words to create an impact with the person we are talking to. Different people may respond more favourably to some words than others.

If you are an advocate of VAK Learning Styles you will know people are either Visual, Auditory or Kinaesthetic Learners/Communicators. So, our final sentence might change accordingly if you are talking to each of these learning styles.

A Visual person would respond better to, *"How does that look?"*

A Kinaesthetic person would respond better to, *"How does that feel?"*

An Auditory person would respond to, *"How does that sound?"*

These are the three main styles of learning and communication which every person fits into – one way or another.

Some people are **Visual learners** and communicators, others prefer **Auditory words** and others like **Kinaesthetic words** to communicate.

These communication styles were introduced by *Walter Burk Barbe and Raymond Swassing; "Teaching Through Modality Strengths" (1979).*

Although people learn in many ways, there is always a dominant way in which people pick up information and knowledge. This also influences the sort of language they use.

A **VISUAL** learning style involves the use of things which are seen, including pictures, diagrams, demonstrations handouts etc. They will use language like:

- "I see that now"
- "Picture this"
- "What's your view on this?"
- "This is what it looks like"
- "Show me"
- "I need to focus on that",
- "It dawned on me",
- "A sight for sore eyes",
- "An eyeful"
- "This is illuminating"
- "Tunnel vision"
- "Bird's eye view"

An **AUDITORY** learning style involves picking up information primarily through the spoken word, sounds and voices.

They will learn best from audios, listening to people and spoken instructions via the telephone. They will use language like:

- "Tell me"
- "It sounds like..."
- "Let's talk it over"
- "As clear as a bell"
- "That resonates with me",
- "As quiet as a mouse"
- "I need to tune in"

A **KINAESTHETIC** learning style involves the preference for personal touch, they like to feel, touch, do practical hands-on skills. They will use language like:

- "Let me try"
- "I feel that's important"
- "Wow, that's heavy"
- "It all boils down to"
- "Feel the pressure"
- "Keep your shirt on"
- "Get a load of this"
- "Heated argument"
- "I feel a bit luke-warm about this"
- "As sharp as a tack"
- "Pull some strings"

How does this help us when dealing with problems with behaviour, attitude and performance? Well, if we use the right words for people to relate to, it means our communication with them will be easier.

In Vivi's case we could have used: *"How does that sound?" "How does that feel?"* or *"How does that look to you?"* depending on her learning/communication style.

How do you know what someone's learning/communication style is?

Just listen to them.

The words will appear.

How else can we use the Focus Technique?

We can use the technique for: **APPRAISAL REVIEWS / PERFORMANCE MANAGEMENT REVIEWS**

The Focus Technique is a fabulous tool to use in an Performance Appraisal/Review when dealing with a staff member who aspires to a higher position but is not quite at the standard yet. This allows the person to focus on the areas they can develop further.

This is achieved by looking at the BIGGER Picture (wide angle) of the position the person aspires to then zooming into the areas where the person needs to develop (with evidence), then back out to the bigger picture again to keep the person focused.

Here is Case Study 2 again, but this time we are going to look at it with a totally different perspective. You will be surprised how looking at the same information with a different perspective can completely alter how you see the situation and the techniques you use.

This time our focus will be on Vivi wanting a promotion, which she has failed to achieve after two attempts.

CASE STUDY 2 - Manager's Viewpoint

Vivi has been with the company for eight years, six of those in this department.

She has applied for promotion several times, but has never been successful, although she is extremely knowledgeable and skilful in the current role.

Recently her attitude has been quite sharp with customers, several complaints have been brought to your attention.

Vivi has become bitter towards others in the team, particularly two younger members she is mentoring.

She has also recently upset other members of the team and is currently unusually lacking enthusiasm.

Vivi's product knowledge and the practical elements of the job cannot be faulted.

She recently wrote a Customer Service training programme for new starters into the department which went down really well.

She would normally have considered her to be really good at her job and has the potential to progress to the next level, but her recent behaviour worries you.

Now let's look at the same case study but from Vivi's viewpoint. Here is how it would go:

CASE STUDY 2 - Vivi's Viewpoint

Vivi feels hard done by, she has given loyal service to the company for eight years, with six in this department alone. On many occasions she has carried the department.

Vivi has applied for promotion on several occasions, but has not been successful.

She feels young upstarts come into the department and go straight into better positions.

She spends much time training and working with new staff in the department, and then they move on.

Vivi doesn't agree with some of the new systems being adopted, and is not happy with the present Manager, but has nowhere else to go.

She has recently had an argument in with a customer on the telephone because the customer was being rude and unreasonable regarding a cancelled project.

Now, we can look at her performance review meeting with her Manager (not "a different approach").

Manager: *"Hi Vivi, firstly can I say I was really impressed with the Customer Service training module you wrote, your knowledge of the systems and processes in this department are second to none.* (START ON A POSITIVE)

Which is why I wanted to talk to you further.

I understand you have been very keen to go for a promotion, and you have applied for such a position several times in the past without success.

What do you think are the skills required for the position of Team Leader?"

(ASK VIVI AND WAIT)

Vivi: *"Well, having great product knowledge and knowledge of the systems is really important."*

Manager: *"Yes, I agree, what other skills are required do you think?"* (WHAT ELSE? WAIT)

Vivi: *"Well, the ability to work well with customers, to be able to work well with the team, and training them to do the job."*

Manager: *"Great. What else?"*

Vivi: *"I suppose to be able to work under pressure is important too."*

Manager: *"Those are fabulous points and in some of those you excel yourself. You have tremendous product and systems knowledge – actually, far better than anyone I know.*

You have developed an amazing Customer Service training package for the new starters in the department, which was put into practice successfully with the last group.

However (ZOOM IN) I want to look at two of those skills you mentioned: your ability to get the best from the team and ability to work under pressure.

Your attitude towards your two mentees, Sash and Yvonne, recently has been worrying (EVIDENCE). You have been short tempered with them and caused one of them to be really upset and was found crying in the ladies' toilets earlier this week.

You have also been quite sharp with some customers recently, one specifically (EVIDENCE) was Mr Evans from Dodge and Co. who said you shouted at him the other week when he complained about a delivery which had not occurred on time.

So, what can we do Vivi, to make sure these situations can be improved to give you a better chance of promotion in the future?"

(LOOK FORWARD NOT BACK, WAIT)

Vivi: *"Well I supposed I get frustrated when the new people do not pick up the systems and procedures as quickly as I think they should. I seem to spend a lot more time with then than I think I should – as a result I get behind with my job, I am sorry for Mr Evans, I think he caught me when I was frustrated."*

Manager: *"So, what can we do in the future Vivi to make sure these things don't happen again?"* (LOOK FORWARD NOT BACK)

Note: the Manager just repeated this, because Vivi did not answer the question. She was asked what we can do to make sure these situations can be improved to give a better chance of promotion in the future. She didn't answer it. She talked about the past situation not a future one. It is always important to listen closely to the answer.

The second time round, Vivi answers the question.

Vivi: *"Well, maybe I need to realise people learn at different rates and not to be frustrated if they take longer to learn than I did. Maybe I could look at different ways to explain methods to them."*

Manager: *"Great, what else?"*

Vivi: *"I could have a one-to-one with them after I have shown them a system to see if they have understood it earlier, rather than wait for them to mess it up."*

(WRITE THE POINTS DOWN ON THE GOAL CHART)

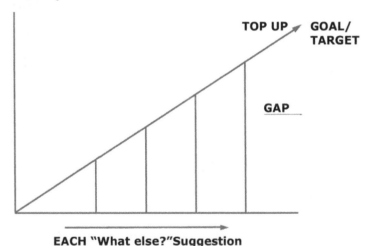

EACH "What else?"Suggestion

Manager: *"Those are two great actions Vivi, what else can we do to make sure you stay on track and do not get frustrated?"*

Vivi: *"Well when I am feeling under pressure, maybe I could just take a deep* *breath, count to 10 and get my focus back before getting on the next call or dealing with the next problem."*

Manager: *"That sounds like an excellent technique, I often do that too. Perhaps, it might help to just take a walk down the corridor or outside to clear your mind and to put things back into an order of priority before you start again? (TOP UP) How does that sound?"* (VAK) Then ask for feedback and get "buy-in".

Vivi: *"Yes that sounds like a good idea, I do fall straight into the next job without taking stock and getting in the right zone, I'll do that."*

Manager: (WIDE ANGLE) *"So, Vivi although I cannot promise you a promotion, I know if you carry on with these changes it will stand you in a much better situation for future promotions as I know you have more experience behind you than the last time you applied."*

Vivi goes out with a plan and more focused on her behaviour.

I love the FOCUS TECHNIQUE when finding solutions.

You can use it for problem behaviour, preparing the person for a different role, or focusing a person's action into a more favourable one.

I love to use it for problems with specific performance, behaviour and attitude, like problems with a customer care focus, teamwork, motivation, communication, or organisational skills.

I love the fact it can show what should be happening – if everything or the person was working effectively, then zoom into the current situation, fix the problem with the person and zoom back out to the wider situation again. This takes the pressure off the person, and puts their focus on a wider result and perspective.

Let's recap the various techniques we saw in the case study you have just read. Remember to watch video 2 to see this in action.

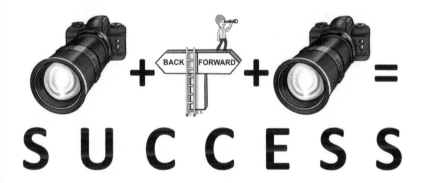

S U C C E S S

Techniques Join

Chapter 8
Too Many Areas to Fix

Now you are getting the idea of how this works, here is another example of some behaviour, attitude or performance which needs to be addressed.

Read Case Study 3 and choose which of the techniques will fit the situation more appropriately, **"LOOK FORWARD NOT BACK"** or **"FOCUS TECHNIQUE"**.

This time we are meeting Victor, instead of Vivi.

After reading it, plan how you would address the situation when you call Victor in *"for a word"*.

CASE STUDY 3 - Manager's Viewpoint

Victor has been with the company for six months; he seems to be a clock-watcher who doesn't want to work overtime even when the department is very busy, and the team has to pull together to meet deadlines.

Victor doesn't seem to talk to you or his colleagues very much and is not interested in other people in the team. He seems to keep himself to himself. He has not attended the wider staff meetings, despite encouragement to do so.

His work is usually quite prompt and accurate, and you have heard he has solved some major anomalies in the accounts recently, which others couldn't identify.

A new computerised administration system has recently been adopted in the department which Victor is struggling to get to grips with.

He is good with customers, and many come through only to him if they have questions, as he is good at problem solving though he has got upset with angry clients when they are on the phone.

The Manager has been in their role for two months and has spent little time with Victor yet.

Victor is a 'BC'. Write your notes here.

Well, which technique will you choose? Which behaviour, attitude, or performance will you address?" Either technique will work successfully. One difficulty we have with this case study is there are so many negatives in Victor's behaviour, performance and attitude, where do we start?

This case study is revealed in Video 3. Use the QR code or go to the website

So where do we start with Victor?

Firstly, we need to start with a positive. There are a couple of positives in his behaviour and performance

He is;

🏃 Prompt and accurate.

🏃 Good with customer problem solving.

Let's start with those first.

Here is my attempt at it. Spot where I go wrong

Manager: "*Hi Victor, lovely to catch up with you, we haven't really seen much of each other since I got here, have we? How's the job going, I hear you are a whizz in spotting the errors in customer paperwork – you fixed one yesterday which no one else saw, well done!* (EVIDENCE)

I wanted to talk to you, Victor, about overtime. As you know the department is run by deadlines in accounts and paperwork and we get really busy at the

end of the month with trying to meet those deadlines, especially if something goes wrong in production and the figures are not available on time. (WIDE ANGLE)

I understand you have not been doing any overtime over the last two months and many of your colleagues have been doing extra because you have not volunteered. (ZOOM IN)

Also, you don't appear to be attending the wider company briefings, especially with the new computerized system, which some people, including you, are struggling with at times. (ZOOM IN)

You seem to be trying to understand it by yourself without talking to the team or asking for help. (ZOOM IN) What can we do, Victor, to make sure these things don't happen in the future?" (LOOK FORWARD NOT BACK).

Whoa, stop there... have you spotted it?

How many things, after a compliment, are we going to hit Victor with?

What if you were in Victor's shoes at this moment? If he is already quiet, he is likely to go further into his shell. If he is at the end of his tether, he may burst!

Can I Have A Word?

Choose What You Need to Fix First

When there are a lot of improvements to cover it is important to identify the main difficulty first.

Tackle one thing at a time and, if necessary, park some minor issues to see how things settle. Chose the actions which have the most impact on the department or job first.

Let's look at the overtime issue, this is causing major difficulties across the department. Many team members are upset with having to put extra hours in when Victor is not taking his fair share, and this is affecting productivity and staff morale. This is our best starting point.

Remember, one step at a time.

Manager: *"I wanted to talk to you, Victor, about overtime. As you know the department is run heavily by deadlines in both accounts and paperwork, and we get really busy at the end of the month when trying to meet those deadlines, especially if something goes wrong in production and the figures are not available on time.*

I understand you have not been doing any overtime over the last two months and many of your colleagues have been doing extra because you have not volunteered.

What can we do, Victor, to make sure you can do the overtime when required?" (LOOK FORWARD NOT BACK)

Or we can use the FOCUS TECHNIQUE

Manager: *"Hi Victor, lovely to catch up with you, we haven't really seen much of each other since I got here, have we? How's the job going, I hear you are a whizz in finding spotting the errors in customer paperwork – you fixed one yesterday which no one else saw, well done!* (EVIDENCE)

(WIDE ANGLE) *One of the key roles we have in this department is getting our accounts and paperwork out to meet the company deadlines. This is absolutely vital if we are going to have the information we need to help with the following months productivity and the production costs, as this affects our cash flow and financial situation. This is crucial to the company's survival and our jobs.*

(ZOOM IN) *However, over the last two months, since I joined the department, I have not seen you do any overtime and when you were on the roster, you took your name off the list twice at the last minute.* (EVIDENCE)

What can we do to ensure you are able to pick up some of the overtime, to help out some of your colleagues from time to time?" (LOOK FORWARD NOT BACK)

WAIT

Be prepared for anything, keep your objective (your bullseye result) in mind at all times.

Victor: *"Well, I can't do overtime, and when you keep putting my name on the list I feel picked on as I can't do overtime and I have to take it off the list. I was never told overtime was compulsory when I joined, and I just can't do it.!"*

Wow, that was unexpected.

It is at this point the Manager feels accused of bullying – there seems to be no solution to Victor's unwillingness to do the overtime.

Many Managers jump in at this point and use the rule book as their shield.

Manager: *"Well if you look at your job description at the bottom it says, 'and any other duties assigned by the Manager...'"*

Please do not go there. You are showing you have lost the battle if you end up referring to the paragraph which always appears at the end of every job description.

You need to know more about this problem, so back up a bit and try to find out what is behind it. It might not be wilful disobedience.

136

Manager: *"Obviously I don't know you very well, only being here myself for a couple of months, it is my fault entirely for not taking the time to get to know you before, so why is it you cannot do overtime?*

Victor: *(after a while of contemplation and silence) "I'm a single dad, have been for the last four months and there is no one to pick my little one up from school every day. I'm the only one, and with all the changes it's been difficult to maintain continuity for her, so when you keep putting my name on the rota, I know I can't do it. So I take it off the day before – so someone else can do it instead."*

Wow, that's a blow.

Did you know this piece of information before you started this conversation? Possibly not! The difficulty with any *"Can I have a word?"* conversation is: we only see things from our own viewpoint. We covered this point in the last case study.

So, what does the Manager do now?

KEEP CONTROL.

Keep the target focused on what needs to be achieved.

It will be important for Victor to take the pressure of the rest off the team by doing some overtime.

This needs to be the new outcome.

We now need to go back to:

Manager: *"I had no idea of your situation Victor, I am so sorry to hear this, you are obviously a very private person and didn't want this known in the department.*

I appreciate that, and the fact you have just confided in me. It is very difficult for many of the team to do the overtime too and many of them have commitments outside of work – which I have to admit they have also struggled with.

What can we do to help take some of the pressure off them from time to time in the future by fitting just a couple over extra hours a month? What can you do?" (LOOK FORWARD NOT BACK)

WAIT

Victor: *"There is no family close to pick her up from school..."*

Manager: *"So what COULD you do, what WOULD you need?"*

Victor: *"Well there is an after-school club but it is booked a month in advance, and I can never be sure when the overtime is expected, it differs every month."*

Manager: *"Okay Victor, what COULD you do?"*

WAIT

I love the question, *"What COULD you do?"* especially if people say things are impossible. Nothing is impossible – there is always something someone COULD do to improve a situation, no matter how small. This helps to create some movement, which is always better than either going backwards or being at an impasse.

Victor: (Pausing) *"I could put her name down for the last two days of each month and see if this fits. It's only for two hours though."*

Manager: *"This sounds like a good start Victor. What else could you do?"*

(Keep focused on the target – we are making some progress)

Victor: *"Well, her Gran is coming over to visit three days a month to help me out, I could ask her to take her to school which would give me an extra couple of hours in the morning and a couple of hours after work – if this helps?"*

Manager: *"I'm sure it would help tremendously, and how about I give you a five weeks' notice about the overtime, so you can make the arrangements with the after-school place and her Gran?*

This would really help the team to schedule their own arrangements rather than having to pick up extra overtime at very short notice, which puts them under even more pressure? How does that look?" (VAK)

Victor: *"I can give it a go and see how it works, as long as it doesn't unsettle her more."*

Manager: *"That's fabulous, yes let's review it in two months to see how it's going, and how much impact it is having on the team. By the way, I take it none of the team know about your home situation.*

It might be worth just sharing it as it may really help with how the job runs and how people can help if you are stuck. They are a nice bunch if you let them be."

Victor: *"Hmmm yes, I'll think about that. You may be right, I never feel like part of the team, as they are all a lot younger than me and go out together some nights. I never feel like I fit in, it's also why I haven't been to the wider meetings as they are always early in the morning or at the end of the day, and I always need to get back to pick my little girl up from school."*

Well, there we have it. We not only know the reason for Victor not doing any overtime, but why he clock watches, doesn't attend the meetings and keeps himself back from the wider team. Bingo! All in one go.

The other difficulties being experienced may melt into insignificance.

WHAT DID YOU SPOT?

Did you spot the HELPING HAND? – "What can we do to help take some of the pressure off them….?" I love the "royal we".

Did you spot the HOWEVER?

Please look at Video 3 to bring this chapter to life and see the impact on both parties.

RECAP
Remember:
Choose your key problem.
Keep your target focused.
Ask for solutions.
Ask "What else?"
Top up.
Get agreement.

C.R.

Chapter 9
Technique 4 - The Happy Burger

Many of you will know this technique from your previous training skills – you might have heard it called a *'praise sandwich'*, we mentioned it briefly in Chapter 6.

The HAPPY BURGER technique starts the *"Can I have a word?"* discussion on a positive note, by noting something good the person has done over the last few weeks. It helps the person realise there is some good in their behaviour and performance; it also helps diffuse a possible explosive situation.

Dale Carnegie says, *'Begin with praise and honest appreciation.'* (Principle 17 in *How to win Friends and Influence People*).

So, if you have met this before, why am I spending MORE time on it?

Well, some people new to management and supervision may not have been trained in this method yet, but others may not have been getting this technique *quite right*.

Managers need to search to find a positive, even if it is difficult. There is always something the team member has done well.

EVIDENCE AND SINCERITY

The power of the Happy Burger (which many people miss) is providing a specific example or evidence with sincerity.

People are not usually expecting praise when they hear "Can I Have A Word?" If all they hear is a glib comment which has no sincerity and no basis of evidence such as "Love the colour of your shoes!" they know you are not being genuine.

Also I have witnessed Managers saying a "good" comment because they think they HAVE TO, rather than it being heartfelt or sincere. This makes the comment sound false, over exaggerated and lacking in clarity.

This results in the staff member feeling it is false, insincere, phoney, artificial, fabricated... how many more synonyms do I need?

If incorrectly done the staff member can read what's coming like a book and it doesn't sound sincere or "heartfelt". When executed badly, the good part sounds false or over exaggerated, the poor bit lacks clarity, and the final good bit is often a repeat of the first.

The result is the staff member feels it's false, insincere, phoney, artificial... how many more synonyms do I need?

What we want to achieve is something which is sincere, honest, genuine, authentic, heartfelt... I like those synonyms better!

How do we achieve this?

Like many other things in this book, it's simple: The power of **EVIDENCE**.

We have encountered **EVIDENCE** previously when we were looking at specific examples of behaviour. Evidence needs to be specific (not woolly), It needs to be both true and relevant to the situation.

Finally, it needs to be *authentic*.

We will now look at CASE Study 4 – with a different Vivi. This case study can be found on Video 4 – but it is best if you watch this after you have finished the book as there are many techniques introduced in this final video. No peaking!! Vivi is an 'AC' who thinks she is an 'AA'.

CASE STUDY 4 - Manager's Viewpoint

"Vivi" has been with the company for eight years. She is a hard worker who is dedicated to doing a good job, but, sometimes at the expense of speed.

Speed is vital to the busy department.

Accuracy is key for her. She will spend a long time making sure a job is done accurately and to the highest quality. These are great traits, but the department needs things done more quickly.

Last month, Vivi spotted a problem with a report before it was published to the Board, which saved an embarrassing situation.

Vivi is often hot-headed and does not get on with some of the others on the team, particularly her younger colleagues, who she feels do not work hard enough, and are lackadaisical in their attitude to work.

She can be temperamental. Her mood swings have caused concern before.

Her department is behind with its production targets, figures and purchasing information and is losing ground, so you need to push things along by getting more productivity.

Here is how the discussion can go with the **HAPPY BURGER**.

Manager: *"Hi Vivi, can I just say I was really impressed by the way you spotted the error in the financials just before our report was going to the Board last month. Several of us had looked over the report, however only you spotted the error, and in time for us to fix it. I really appreciate your effort. It saved a lot of extra work, and personally helped me to look at the system again."*

Or, to make it less sincere you can omit the evidence bits:

Manager: *"Hi Vivi, you did a great job on the Board report last month."*

See the difference?

If you are going to compliment someone, make it *REAL* and sincere. Use **Evidence**, and to make it even better, say what it has meant for you.

We started the conversation with a compliment. This needs to be immediate! It needs to be done virtually the second the staff member has walked in, even before you have directed her/him to sit down.

Why So Soon?

This is because we want them to think it's the most important thing we need to say, and we are eager to share it.

If we say, *"Hello Vivi, thank you for coming in, please take a seat..."* we have lost all the impetus for surprise and her IMPENDING DOOM thoughts can start to emerge.

Get Evidence

Remember most people will feel worried, nervous anxious before they walk in, so we need to jolt them out of this feeling the second they walk through the door.

This means as a Manager you need to prepare this piece of EVIDENCE in advance and deliver it sincerely.

What if no one has a good piece of behaviour to start with? Then you are not looking hard enough. Everyone has done something well at some time!

Once we have started with the GOOD thing the person has done recently, with EVIDENCE, we can then get into the MEAT of our HAPPY BURGER. We start this with:

Always end the interview with another strength /good comment. I suggest you watch this on Video after reading this chapter. This reminds me to tell you about thanking people. We do this every day, but do we do it well or in the right way to create the right level of impact?

Giving Thanks and Appreciation

Many people think saying "thanks" when appreciating someone's work is enough.

Over the years, I realised there are many levels of giving thanks before we hit the TARGET. The target is the central point where the person being thanked really **feels** the appreciation at an emotional level.

This is the MOST POWERFUL thanks of all.

Maybe you can reflect on those situations in the past where the *"thanks"* you received was shallow and meaningless, or maybe when someone said something to you in gratitude and it rocked you in your boots. WOW!

There are actually four levels of appreciation. This section alone will change your life and the lives of others forever."

LEVEL 1 Appreciation

We often use the term, *"Thanks,"* or *"Thanks for that,"* when someone has done something for us. This may be nice, but does it match the level of effort a person has put into the task?

Here is an example:

- Someone passes you the salt at the dinner table without you asking for it. *"Thanks"* or *"Thanks for that"* will be great.

- Someone brings you in a hot drink after you have been on three long back-to-back Zoom meetings, and they have just come back in from a long commute after a tiring day. *"Thanks"* just doesn't stand up, as the amount of effort and thought which has gone into the act is far bigger than the level of thanks received.

You will know what I mean when someone at work has said, *"Thanks for that"* after you have slaved over a report for hours. It just doesn't cut it. You feel like muttering something under your breath, or maybe making a naughty gesture behind their back!

Often when they say, *"Thanks"* they do so without any direct eye contact.

Instead of feeling appreciated the person's actions have appeared shallow and meaningless to them. This can even feel demotivating, like, *"Why should I bother?"*

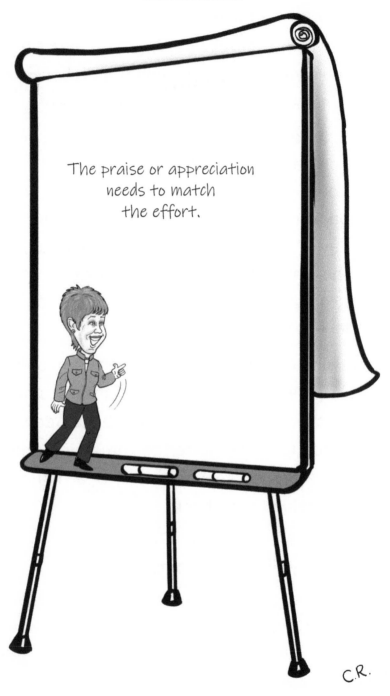

The praise or appreciation
needs to match
the effort.

C.R.

LEVEL 2 Appreciation

"Thank you" **✛** what you are thanking them for. Here is an example:

"Thanks for the drink, I was really parched and didn't get the chance to grab one earlier," while looking directly at the person and maybe giving them a smile.

That's better. Now they know what you are thanking them for, and the body language matches the words. This may be all that is required for this level of help.

The other person may now reply, *"That's OK, I thought you might have been busy"* and they will feel their efforts have been appreciated. Sometimes they just say, *"That's okay"* and nod appreciatively.

In a work environment, a Level 2 appreciation may be, *"Thanks for collecting those tools for me, it saved me quite a bit of time."* Again, you said thank you and why you are thanking them. *"No probs"* comes the reply. Job done.

LEVEL 3 Appreciation

Can we go even further in appreciation? Oh yes!

✛ Thank you.

✛ What you are thanking them for.

What it has meant for you.

153

This is an amazing way to give credit where credit is due. This is how it sounds:

"Thank you for collecting those tools for me, it saved me a lot of time and it really helped me get the machine to the customer in good time."

The answer then comes back: *"It was no problem, I was pleased to help."*

Here is another:

"Thank you so much for staying late last night, the work really needed to be finished and it meant I could get to Kelly's school concert. I missed it last time."

This is one of the sincerest ways to say thank you I know. It gives the amount of praise required for the task, identifies their contribution, and shows how it impacted on you, the team, the company etc.

Can you do better?

Well you can, Oh yes.

LEVEL 4 Appreciation - The Wow Factor!

This level of appreciation really hits the sweet spot.

This is the point by which a person either silently in their head, or openly says, ***"WOW"***.

It happens when the appreciation comes from an unexpected place, like a higher boss, or a third party.

It goes like this:

"I have just heard in the management meeting, you stayed behind two nights running this week to get the paperwork and parts finished for the overseas conference. Everything got there and was set up without a hitch, they were very grateful. Thank you."

 "Wow, I didn't think they would even know!"
BULLS EYE!

At this level it is not you saying thank you for something they have done - it is where their work and effort is appreciated by a higher body or an outside source like a customer.

Here is another:

"I have just received a fabulous email from ABC Engineering. They were really impressed by the way you dealt with their problem of a missing part and rectified it within a day. They had a major customer waiting and they were able to fulfil a tight deadline as a result. Thank you."

The importance of this is its sincerity. It has real evidence and comes from an external source.

Overleaf there is a diagram where you can see the "Thanks" only just touches the outer edge of the target.

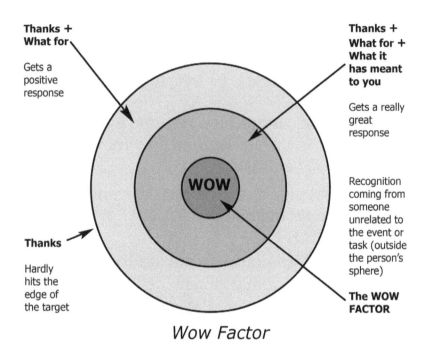

Thanks +
What for

Gets a
positive
response

Thanks +
What for +
What it
has meant
to you

Gets a really
great
response

Recognition
coming from
someone
unrelated to
the event or
task (outside
the person's
sphere)

Thanks

Hardly
hits the
edge of
the target

The WOW
FACTOR

Wow Factor

Remember, sincerity is a key word here. Whenever we compliment someone, we need to make it sincere. This means we give eye contact, positive body language and EVIDENCE.

When the Manager said,

"Hi Vivi, can I just say, I was really impressed by the way you spotted the error in the financials just before our report was going to the Board last month. Several of us had looked over the report, only you spotted the error, and, in time for us to fix it. I really appreciated it. It saved a lot of extra work, and personally helped me to relook at the system again".

This is Level 3 Appreciation

This points out to the staff member is there is some or a lot of good in what they are doing, and you appreciate the effort.

Sometimes Managers and Supervisors (and even parents, friends, partners or spouses) fail to show appreciation for the things people have done.

We often take people for granted.

Who could you show appreciation for today? What difference would it make to them – the receiver, and to you – the giver?

Let's get back to Vivi and her over exuberance with accuracy.

Why Praise Again? (The topping of the HAPPY BURGER)

In the second visit to the PRAISE part of the HAPPY BURGER, it is important that the second and final PRAISE is something TOTALLY different from the first.

Remember, it has to be real, sincere, totally meaningful and work related.

So to recap, we started with something GOOD the person has done (with EVIDENCE).

We then got to the 'meat' of the discussion.

We finish off with another GOOD thing the person has done.

What we want is the team member to feel really good about themselves when they walk out of the room, as they did when they walked in, when we hit them with the first sincere praise.

When they walk out of the meeting, yes, they may have had an issue addressed, but it was sandwiched between two good things they have done. Things which have been recognised.

This way they are less inclined to go out of the room and infect other people.

Now, let's look at how all the conversation with Vivi might go:

Manager: *"Hi Vivi, can I just say I was really impressed by the way you spotted the error in the financials just before our report was going to the Board last month. Several of us had looked over the report, only you spotted the error, and, in time for us to fix it. I really appreciate it.*

It saved a lot of extra work, and personally helped me to relook at the system again". (HAPPY BURGER)

Vivi: *"Oh that's fine, I have a talent for these things. Glad you fixed it in time."*

Manager: (FOCUS TECHNIQUE) *"As you know our department has a lot of responsibility to provide accurate and timely information to the whole company so it can make its decisions in terms of purchasing, allocation of resources and* financial decisions, and in today's difficult economic market with inflation rising by the second it is important to get accurate financial information quickly.

(ZOOM IN) *However, over the month and particularly over the last two weeks when the Sales and Finance teams have had to make very fast decisions, there has always been a delay from you and your section in getting the information to them.*

(EVIDENCE). *I am particularly talking about two weeks ago when the fuel rates and inflation hit all at the same time – the Board had some major decisions on purchasing to make ahead of some of the changes, they asked six times for the information they needed, and there was a major delay on your part. This wasn't the first time.*

I know accuracy is really important to you, but it can't be totally at the expense of timeliness. What can we do to make sure this doesn't happen again?" (LOOK FORWARD NOT BACK)

Vivi: *"Well accuracy is totally important, as I see it. If you want figures which are meaningless ask the rest of the team to do it - especially the younger ones, as they are so slapdash. I would like to drill them into shape. I have always wanted to lead*

*the team. They would soon be accurate.
I don't know why some of them are still
here!"*

Vivi is using a great **deflection tool**. She
is deflecting the issue from herself to others.
Moving the blame to others is useful as the
Manager cannot deal with it immediately. Watch
out for this type of response. It is a common
tool. In this case study, you will see it is the
Managers responsibility to deal with issues
relating to the performance of other staff, not
Vivi's.

By bringing other people into the situation
they think the Manager might be put off guard
and go down a different track. Clever Vivi.

Manager: *"I am well aware that some of
the younger members have a lot to learn
yet, and maybe your expertise might be
of valuable help to them in the future.*

*I will address the situation with the
younger team members, however, we
need to address what you can do to
provide accurate figures more quickly
when required. What can you do to make
sure you get a better balance between
accuracy and speed?"* (LOOK FORWARD
NOT BACK again to reiterate and to keep
on the subject)

Vivi: *"Well, I could make sure the data
I have is up to date before I start so the*

Chapter 9: Technique 4 - The Happy Burger

spreadsheets are accurate."

Manager: *"That's a great idea Vivi, what else could you do?"*

Vivi: *"I could run the data off in the quick run and check it meets the percentage levels required for profitability."*

Manager: *"Sounds good, what else could you do? I appreciate it is hard for you."*

Vivi: *"Well I could check the data three times before sending it to the Board."*

Manager: *"How many times do you usually check it?"*

Vivi: *"Generally six or seven."*

Manager: *"And how many times after the third check have you ever found anomalies?*

Vivi: *"Well... none."*

Manager: *"So Vivi, if you make sure you check the spreadsheet data is correct first, you make sure the percentage profitability levels are OK and you only need to check three times. I am sure the speed of response for you to the Board will be a lot faster, and also the accuracy level will be up to your standards. How does that sound?"* (PLAN OF ACTION)

Vivi: *"Yes that sounds ok, I'll give it a go. It won't be easy though"*

161

Manager: *"And Vivi before you go, the new report format as gone down a treat with the Board, they loved the new style; it has made it much easier to read and understand. Well done!"* (HAPPY BURGER... seeded part!)

See that was easy.

Before we go onto the final technique in this book, I would like to spend a little time on something which totally changed our working lives, our home lives and the way we operated; the global pandemic.

The techniques in this book are all well and good in the workplace, but what if the workplace changed? What if the workplace changed forever?

Chapter 10
During the Global Pandemic

When the Global pandemic hit, much of the world went into lockdown. People started to work from home, there was concern about how they would cope with working from home, and how they would work unsupervised.

The Press posted pictures of people lazing about in their pyjamas or sitting outside in the garden during the hot weather while supposedly working from home. The reality was very different for many people whose working life was rocked and turned upside down.

On top of home-working many people faced the additional challenge of home-schooling. Some households had two or three people trying to work on the same computer at the same time.

Many people I know had to work on laptops in their bedrooms, or on makeshift desks. The desks, chairs, and computers were, inappropriate for working full days, day after day. The dining room or kitchen table became the office, with family members and pets passing through. There was little opportunity for confidentiality.

It was initially difficult for companies to monitor home working in the same way they could with someone working in an office.

How was home working going to affect performance, customer service, attendance, productivity? The questions loomed.

The global pandemic changed the way many organisations had to deal with performance, attitude and behaviour in the workplace.

This has special significance in an article by *Kessler Kalim*, Director of HR at The London School of Hygiene and Tropical Medicine who, on Global Performance Management, asked,

"Given that a company's workforce now has a significant proportion of virtual and freelance workers, how should performance management include them?"

He goes on to say: *"An effective and inclusive performance management framework should not detrimentally affect any type of worker, irrespective of whether they are based in the head office, or a remote location on the other side of the world.*

The culture of performance management in an organisation, embraced and led by senior management, should transcend geographical location. In an age of

globalization, remote working and the plethora of available technologies, engaging with virtual and freelance workers has never been easier. Ensuring these groups of workers and their Managers buy into the performance management culture is key."

In his final point, he says, *"I am a passionate advocate for continuous discussion and dialogue on performance and development. For a good Manager, effective performance discussions occur daily."*

The key to all areas of performance management is the CULTURE of the organisation. There needs to be an effective way to discuss, appraise and review staff at any time regardless of their proximity to the office. I love the quotation: *"For a good Manager, effective performance discussions occur daily."*

This is totally congruent with the messages in this book. Most Managers and Directors I have met have viewed Appraisals and Performance Reviews as a chore to be done once a year, and put back in the drawer.

So, during lockdown, how did Managers review performance, attitude, and behaviour? What happened in your organisation?

If someone was not performing to the standard required, had a poor attitude, or behaved in the wrong way, how did companies pick this up and deal with it during a pandemic?

During the Pandemic period, and immediately after, I talked to Managers and staff from companies across different sectors to establish how they were dealing with performance, behaviour, and attitude in the 'homeplace', and how staff felt their work was being supervised.

The results were amazing.

I have purposely not mentioned names or specific organisations in my analysis.

Company Examples

I found most staff members working from home actually put MORE hours in than was expected of them.

People often had to alter their working day due to family commitments, but made up time. Many made up MORE time!

The organisations initially reported, 'many people were working in very difficult conditions, ill-equipped to do their job, but managed to do the best they could.'

My brother, in fact, spent over two years sitting on a dining chair in the kitchen. He is still sitting in these conditions now.

The correct equipment, chair, workstation and IT set-ups were often not in place, and as such, many longer-term ergonomic difficulties will no doubt emerge.

When the children were home schooling, parents had to balance work, childcare and education.

With all this happening, with no planning or preparation, how did staff and Managers cope with this difficult period?

Two companies I spoke to immediately conducted self-assessments with their staff to establish what they needed to operate effectively and provided the equipment required as quickly as possible. Staff were also asked if it was feasible for them to work from home.

On monitoring their team, one Manager said: *"The systems told us the progress of projects through spreadsheets and project management systems. The Supervisors logged into the servers from home each day, and I had daily and weekly calls with each of them both as teams and 1-to-1's".*

Another Manager said: *"People reacted differently to working from home. We had to do a lot of training for staff, and students in the use of Microsoft Teams® to communicate effectively. Initially video calls were scary for everyone."*

Where staff were furloughed (the system where Government paid part of a person's wages to employers when a person couldn't work, without losing their employment) there

Zoom Meeting Request

were weekly 1-to-1s and *'keep in touch'* Zoom meetings and telephone calls.

The success of the businesses, in my survey, was determined by the amount of communication they had with their teams during the long lockdown period. One Manager said, *"In the weekly 1-to-1s I could reassure the team and check on their mental health. The priority for me was: they were not worried when we eventually started a staggered return to work."*

In one organisation, teams were encouraged to log off the system on Friday afternoons, to have a longer weekend with family. The company realised how difficult it was working from home for some of them.

All the companies reported the same key activity. Daily and weekly Zoom calls which allowed Managers to assess how people were doing, and they could start to see when difficulties or frustration was setting in. If frustration, or anxiety affected them, the staff members were advised to log off and go and take a lovely walk and take a break.

Where it was realised that staff were struggling, the Managers arranged to *"Have a word"* generally over Teams® or Zoom®. Some Managers told me they had to work out different working hours with the staff member so the family commitments could be completed positively and the job could get done to a high level. This new work - life balance worked in everyone's favour.

So, even during the Pandemic whilst home working, people were asked to set up Zoom calls to *"Have a word."*

It was evident where companies had regular 1-to-1's with staff it made the communication and situation seem normal. This normality created certainty and an opening up of relationships.

This was not the case for other people in my survey. The message, *"Can you attend a Zoom?"* did not always create a smile. Even if there was nothing wrong people still felt the fear and worry of the Zoom meeting just like they would if the Manager stood outside the office and said, *"Can I have a word?"*

One Manager commented, *"The most important thing was to build was trust. We needed to trust staff and staff needed to trust us; a few times they had meetings in pairs so people could work together and not feel isolated.*

A couple of people found working from home a culture shock and took a while find their own work discipline. Sadly, one person did not manage to work from home and asked to leave."

How did Managers realised people were struggling? Often people were slower to answer email or phone calls, and other difficulties were noticeable over Zoom® meetings

One Manager said, *The key was understanding the person, being aware of the non verbal signals and keeping communication open. The communication was not all about work it was important to chat about the family, weekend, and what people were doing.*

During this period, many Managers learned the value of; face to face contact and importance of body language.

One discussion with an HR consultant, who worked with many organisations during the Pandemic period, revealed that companies who did not have systems in place struggled to monitor performance. Their only method of monitoring much of the daily performance was through weekly 1 to 1 meeting on Zoom.

What made the *"having a word"* discussion even more difficult was not knowing if the conversation was confidential, and if anyone else was listening in, as you couldn't see anyone but the person on Zoom, and the phone calls could be on loudspeaker.

"Communication, observation, and understanding the team, and their motivations and difficulties, was the key to maintaining performance and achieving our individual and collective goals. Having those conversations to keep people

going and focused during those difficult times was essential", said one Manager.

In summary, during the Global Pandemic period the organisations I interviewed learned new skills to ensure performance, behaviour and attitudes were upheld.

They all learned to communicate more with their teams to judge motivation levels, and spot difficulties, often not by statistics or systems, but by observing body language and importantly the unsaid word.

They became more observant and understanding of their people, dealt with situations more quickly to stop them festering, and nipped difficulties in the bud before they got out of control.

What has this taught us?

- Get to know your people.
- Communicate often.
- Understand their motivations, practises, and skill sets.
- When there is an issue, don't be like Gollum!
- Act quickly and effectively to identify the problem.
- Use direct evidence, not hearsay.
- "Look Forward not Back" to create future solutions.

- Monitor and observe; not just statistics and information but the person, their moods, and the spoken and unspoken word.

- Follow up, keep them on track.

- Never be afraid to talk.

The pandemic taught us a lot about people management and the importance of regular, meaningful communication, monitoring not only the performance of practical things but the importance of the unspoken word – just as much as the spoken word.

Indeed, this realisation only strengthens the importance of techniques you have already discovered.

In my manufacturing business, *HydroVeg Kits*, I plant little seedlings in their pots and place them in their own home in the hydroponic garden kit. I apply water, nutrients and switch on the pump.

My kits are all about easy gardening, but I still need to watch over them, check their growth is going to plan, and monitor that they are blooming. Sometimes the cheeky vegetables grow enormous roots which need a haircut.

Without the haircut the roots can stop the flow of water, which affects all the other plants and the pump. Some plants won't get water, and others will get too much as the water will not flow effectively as the big roots slow it down or even stop it.

Why am I telling you this?

It is because everything we do has a cause and effect. Just popping my seedlings in their pots in the *HydroVeg Kit* will not give me fresh healthy vegetables. The plants need an amount of care and nurturing, for me to address the problems they face, and I need to understand the knock-on effect one plant may have on another... or on all of them.

If I stopped going into my garden and checking on their welfare, I would have no tomatoes, broccoli, courgettes or aubergines. Little Cabbage Whites would have eaten all my greens.

Management is just like this. Just having staff doesn't mean all your targets are met, customers and suppliers are happy, or your productivity and profitability targets are met.

Every person, system and process needs to be nurtured and cared for. This is what the companies I interviewed taught me. They had to be more mindful of the systems, equipment, and procedures. They needed to innovate, adapt and integrate. They needed to get in tune with their people to enable them to function, grow and bloom.

What was realised throughout the pandemic period was the importance of communication, understanding people, and never leaving things to chance but instead - following up.

Managers made sure people were doing the right things, and any difficulties were dealt with quickly before they spread and affected other things. Following up with team members was essential. They couldn't leave things to chance.

This brings up aptly to the next technique in the book the importance of the "FOLLOW UP".

Setting off on a course of action is important. Even more important is keeping on course, regardless of what may come your way. My favourite quote of all times comes from Jim Rohn, *The same wind blows on us all: the winds of disaster, opportunity and change. Therefore, it is not the blowing of the wind, but the setting of the sails that will determine our direction in life."*

Starting a new action or behaviour is only the first step. The action or behaviour needs to be continued, developed, re-evaluated and perfected.

So, as a Manager it is important you follow up – to keep that progress moving in the right direction, and where necessary to adjust and re-set the sails to achieve the result.

"The same wind blows on us all: the winds of disaster, opportunity and change. Therefore, it is not the blowing of the wind, but the setting of the sails that will determine our direction in life."

Jim Rohn

Chapter 11
Technique 5 – The Follow Up

When talking to Managers one of the things they hate just as much as the "Having a word" is following the meeting up afterwards.

When I ask why, they tell me it's like they are *"keeping their eye on the person"* and openly monitoring them.

They tell me they feel like is a form of bullying or spying.

Staff members tell me they feel its like *"Big Brother is watching them"* and they feel *"picked on"* and *"not trusted"*.

FOLLOW UP is an essential part of dealing with behaviour, attitude or performance issues.

As Managers you can't just hope the problem has been fixed and hope it never darkens your doors again.

If the behaviour or attitude has been a longstanding issue, it will not just go away after one discussion – no matter how good a manager you are, and no matter how well you followed the techniques in this book.

It is now time to look at **HOW to make sure the performance, behaviour, or attitude improves, reduces or vanishes as needed.**

FOLLOW UP needn't be nasty, vindictive, or bullying. Instead, it should be positive, perfectly timed and totally necessary.

Remember a few case studies ago the Manager told Vivi they would review their discussion and actions in three months; with Victor it was two months. This is a very important aspect of *"having a word"*.

If we don't follow up, the staff member can think, we don't care, or the issue is not important enough. They think we have forgotten what we talked about and whatever they do, no-one is interested.

They are so wrong! Why don't Managers follow up? It's for all the scary reasons we mentioned at the start of the Chapter, but also because they are busy, new priorities take over... STUFF HAPPENS.

Is this a good excuse? No! Regardless of all the pressures of life and work following up on performance, behaviour or attitude discussions is a must.

There are two stages to the FOLLOW UP:

The first stage is letting the team member know you are going to follow up and get their agreement.

Let's go back to Vivi's last encounter and see

how it sounds.

Manager: *"OK, So Vivi, if you make sure you check the spreadsheet data is correct first, you make sure the percentage profitability levels are OK and you only check three times, I am sure not only will the response from you to the Board be a lot faster, but the accuracy level will be up to your standards. How does that sound?"*

Vivi: *"Yes that sounds OK, I'll give it a go. It won't be easy though."*

Manager: *"How about we review the situation in a month to see how the changes are working?"*

Vivi: *"Yes that sounds OK."*

It was simple to let Vivi know her Manager would review the situation in a month. The end of the discussion linked directly to setting up a review. Both parties agreed. It was all out in the open, and both will be **expecting** it to happen, particularly Vivi.

It is so easy for Managers after *"Having that word"* to think: *"Thank goodness that's over and I won't have to deal with it again!"* and brush it under the carpet.

If you do this, the problem will not go away and - dealing with it in the future will be even harder.

The difficulty of a review is actually having the review.

Life, work, business demands all get in the way, and before you know it, the review time has come and gone.

I remember as a Training Manager, I had designed and developed a new performance appraisal system. It took me ages to design it, meeting the demands of an extremely busy company with offices all over the UK and overseas.

After the design work, I started to train the Managers in the new system.

I could tell immediately which Managers would follow the system and run exceptional appraisal reviews.

I was right: the sales and customer service departments had Managers who were hot on communication, feedback, training and measuring performance.

All their reviews were done and follow up reviews not only planned but actioned.

The accounts and IT department and a few others struggled to get their reviews completed, rarely did a follow up. By the next year very few reviews had been completed. How could they run an effective performance review the next year?

They just couldn't see the value. But where were all the performance difficulties hiding? You guessed! – it was in those departments.

Then, after spending months designing and testing the new performance review system and training all the Managers and Supervisors across the company both in the UK and overseas, it came to the day of my appraisal review.

I waited expectantly. I had gone to bed early the night before, awoke early with anticipation, excitement, and a little apprehensive.

My appraisal was due at 11am. I looked into the HR Directors office and she was busy on the phone, so I sat back down. Minutes later I popped up again to see if she was free. This carried on for over two hours, when she suddenly shouted me in,

"What's with all this peering into my office all morning? Every time I looked up you were there!"

"It's my appraisal review," I said, *"It was scheduled for 11am and it's 2.45pm now."*

She responded with, *"Well, I just haven't got time, and I am away for the rest of the week. It will just have to wait."*

Guess what? I never did get the appraisal/ performance review. How do you think I felt after creating, embedding and managing a company wide – in fact worldwide system – and beings one of the few people in the company to never actually experience it myself?

I felt worthless, my work was devalued and I saw how important I was in my Manager's eyes.

I have just been talking about performance reviews here, not necessarily the *"Can I have a word"* discussions, but in reality it's all the same thing: The meeting between two people to review performance, behaviour and attitude and to create a plan forward.

So, everything we have talked about in the book about *"having a word"*, and the techniques involved, are EXACTLY the same when conducting an annual performance review.

For these reviews, you need to understand the job, the relationships, and the performance levels: establish evidence and identify gaps; and adapt or change what is required so you can plan for the future.

Once the review is completed, what happens to it? Does it go in a file, only to be pulled out at the last minute before the next annual review or is it a continuous working document which can alter and evolve through the year?

I bet if I was to check out many of your systems, the answer would be the former.

What a waste of time, effort and energy.

Do It – Review It!

The second stage of the FOLLOW UP is you need to observe how those changes you both discussed and agree are progressing.

I am not talking about being on someone's back or monitoring openly but keeping an eye out and – being more aware of what is happening.

This takes me to my final technique, **TWO EARS**.

Technique: Two Ears

Good Ear and Bad Ear

Chapter 12
Technique 6 – Two Ears

What is this about? This is about overseeing, noticing, watching the performance, behaviour or attitude you and the staff member agreed upon.

It is a positive action, so subtle in its execution the staff member hardly notices.

I love this technique as it gives immediate praise to a person for doing the things they suggested and can be a gentle reminder of actions they said they would take. It is non-confrontational and creates lasting results.

Having two ears are not to hear through but to talk into!

In this technique, you feed back information to the team member in a timely way whenever they are either doing the RIGHT THING or the WRONG THING.

Dale Carnegie uses this principle, *'Praise the slightest improvement and praise every improvement. Be 'hearty' in your approbation and lavish in your praise.' (Principle 27 in How to Win Friends and Influence People).*

At the end of this chapter you can watch Video 4 which takes you from The HAPPY BURGER, to FOLLOW UP and onto TWO EARS, but be patient, read to the end of this chapter first.

Doing the Right Thing – The Good Ear

When you have discussed and agreed with the staff member a plan and the way forward. It is important they put the plan into action.

During the following days and weeks, and definitely before your agreed review, keep an interested and watchful eye on the staff member and note them doing what was agreed.

For Vivi, it might be she is taking more time with the new people in the team, or completing work quicker. For Victor it might be signing up for some overtime, or attending a department meeting. In fact, it can be anything you discussed, and they agreed they would do.

I mention the book *Zapp!!* once more as it is one of the best management books I have ever read. It says, *"People learn faster from successes than failures."*

Observe and quietly with no fuss, approach the person about one of the positive things you have seen them do, or know they have done, and in their good ear (it doesn't physically matter which one) just let them know you are pleased to see what they are doing.

Here is an example:

Manager: (Whisper) *"Great to see your name on the overtime rota for the second week running Victor, I know how hard it is for you, but I really appreciate the effort you have shown. Well done."*

Can you see how nice this is? Imagine Victor getting this message quietly in his ear. He might smile, nod, or say thank you. Regardless of what he does, he has taken the comment in and internalised it.

He certainly isn't going to jump round the office doing cartwheels. The technique relies on the quietness and the personal nature of the feedback.

Your comment needs to be sincere and reflect the discussion you had.

Here are some for Vivi:

Manager: (Whisper) *"I have just been up to department Z, and they are all fully engaged in your next project. Well done, you have really got them motivated."*

"I have seen you really engaging with the younger team members over the last few days, you seem to be getting along and they seem to be picking things up more quickly. Carry on with your approach, it seems to be working."

The benefit of this is Vivi and Victor know you are interested in them improving after the chat. They will be pleased you have spotted them putting their solutions into action, and you have taken the time to mention it.

The fact you are not making a scene is also great, as no-one except the two of you, needs to know about "the word" you had, or that you have been watching their success.

This is a really fabulous way to keep people on the RIGHT TRACK once they have started to move forward.

I liken it to the approach we would have with a toddler who is just taking their first steps. We would be encouraging, smiling, reassuring and urging them on, *"Come on that's right, good girl. You can do it, yes!"*

Sometimes though, the agreed action may not be happening the way you had both envisaged. This is when we need the OTHER ear.

Doing the Wrong Thing – The Bad Ear

If the person is not following the plan of action you had both agreed to in the meeting, you will need to address this quietly with no fuss into their BAD EAR.

Here is how this might go with Victor.

Manager: (Whisper) *"Victor, remember you said you would manage to get at least one overtime session in this month – I know it's difficult but it would really help the team."*

For Vivi it would be:

Manager: (Whisper) *"Remember to count to 10 and have a walk if you start to feel stressed, you need to keep your composure if you are going to effectively lead the team."*

Or

Manager: (Whisper) *"Vivi, remember you said you would do less check on the data so it would speed up the information you need for the Board meeting? Keep this in mind."*

When Would We Do This Bad Ear Process?

If someone is:

- Not quite on the right track.
- Not started their action yet. Or,
- Started but seems to have drifted back into previous behaviour, attitude or performance.

The BAD EAR method gets them back on track by nudging the behaviour back to where it should be. It might only need a very slight nudge to put it back on track.

If someone hasn't made a start on their actions yet, or you have seen no evidence of a change in behaviour, performance, or attitude, the BAD EAR can be the conduit for change.

If the staff member made some progress but it has stopped, it is a great reminder to enable progress moving again.

The fact you are bringing it up focusses their attention on what needs to change. It also sends them the message that you **are** watching them with interest, you want them to succeed - and if they are not doing what they had agreed as a solution you are aware of it.

Let's get back to the toddler taking its first steps. If you said, *"No, that's not right, your steps are too small, you are too slow, that's rubbish,"* then the child will undoubtedly sit down and refuse to move. It may well be a while before they attempt to walk again.

This technique is carried out softly, with no fuss and is a private conversation.

If someone is doing the right thing and following the plan you both agreed then they will be pleased to see that you are noticing, and the praise helps to cement the good actions. If we get praised for doing something right, we will do it right **more often**. As with children, if we praise them for tidying their room they will respond positively and do more of it.

We all love praise and recognition. It energises us and we do **more** of the right things. It shows our boss, parent, or coach is seeing us doing the right things and is recognising our efforts. It keeps the train on the right track and moving forward. Forward momentum is the goal.

If the person thinks their efforts are not being noticed, they will start to fall back into their old ways – thinking even though they are doing well, no one sees or even cares.

If the person is not on the right track or has slipped off it, this gentle reminder in their ear nudges them back on track to start or continue their journey.

Because you are dealing with it quietly (no fuss and without anyone else hearing) it allows the staff member to alter their actions without people noticing. BUT they know you haven't forgotten and are still on their case (in a nice way).

The TWO EAR approach allows the Manager or Supervisor to keep the momentum going or gets the action started without the need to be monitoring openly or negatively. If the staff member thinks you are interested enough to comment, it helps to keep them on track.

This also helps the review meeting later, as they know they have been either doing the RIGHT or WRONG thing way in advance of the review date, so it forms part of the process.

The review meeting should NOT bring up

any surprises if you are doing the TWO EARS correctly.

The other reason this is a superb technique is it takes the difficulty out of monitoring openly and the person thinking they are being picked on or bullied. Although you are mentioning it, you are only talking about what they *"said and agreed to"* and you are not making a fuss – it's just a gentle reminder.

I love this approach, and when you get it right, you will find it's a fabulous way to give praise to people who are doing a great job **every** day.

Turn Daily Practice to Culture Change

Why not turn this daily practice of giving feedback and appreciation into a culture change throughout the organisation, family or team?"

In fact, the good ear is a lovely way of showing Level 2 and 3 Appreciation. Simply add evidence to turn a Level 2 Appreciation into a Level 3.

Observe other teams and listen out for good things being said by other Managers, Directors, customers and suppliers so you can share Level 4 Appreciation, the **Wow Factor**. This could be inspirational.

> Imagine, someone has just had a dealt with a call from a difficult client really well. The GOOD EAR can pop in virtually immediately or at a suitable time after and show the team member you not only noticed, but have taken time out to comment. How

motivational is this?

If the person has just dealt with a call, in a less positive way, a little word in the BAD EAR immediately nudges the staff member back on the right track, focused and eager to improve.

If we did the TWO EARS technique more often maybe we wouldn't need to call someone in to have a "Have a word". What a fabulous thought!

- Imagine, a team where the Manager created little moments of **MAGICAL** every day. What a wonderful place to work!

- Imagine a whole company having those MAGIC moments each and every day. What motivation, drive and impetus the company would have to develop, grow and thrive.

- Imagine a place where the whole company culture focused on excellence, accomplishment and fulfilment.

- Imagine this happening at home, at the sports club, with the teenagers, with the family, at school.

All because we have **TWO EARS**.

People, you know, can be difficult beings. We have much to learn about human relationships. We are always learning and exploring. We can use new and simple techniques to make the future path less rocky.

I trust this book with its six techniques has helped you deal with those rocky pathways and allow you smooth out a new route. Maybe it's the start of a new beginning...imagine!

Fun Training on AA, AB Method

Resources and References

Resources

VIDEO CONTENT

Each case study and all six techniques can be viewed on video at www.suetonks.com. Just follow the links.

The Videos will cover the following areas.

Video 1 covers:
- Case Study 1
- "The Path of Impending Doom"
- "The Deep Pit of What Happened"
- Technique 1 "LOOK FORWARD NOT BACK"
- Technique 2 "WHAT ELSE?"

Video 2 covers:
- Case Study 2
- Technique 3 "THE FOCUS TECHNIQUE"

Video 3 covers:
- Case Study 3
- Technique 3 "THE FOCUS TECHNIQUE (continued)

Video 4 covers:
- Case Study 4
- Technique 4 "THE HAPPY BURGER"
- Technique 5 "FOLLOW UP"
- Technique 6 "TWO EARS"

Watching the videos for "Can I Have a Word?"

I am excited to dovetail this book with four videos which cover the key techniques. They will bring the book to life and show you how words create the emotions and feelings.

To watch the videos you can either scan each QR code which will take you to each video in turn. Alternatively you can watch them on my Website www.suetonks.com and follow the links.

Happy watching.

Video 1

Video 2

Video 3

Video 4

References

Books

Byham, William C and Cox, Jeff, *Zapp! The Lightning of Empowerment: How to Improve Quality, Productivity, and Employee Satisfaction*, (Ballantine Books) 1998

Carnegie, Dale, *How to Win Friends and Influence People,* (Vermilion; New Ed edition) 2006

Redfield, James, *The Celestine Prophecy: How to Refresh your Approach to Tomorrow with a New Understanding, Energy and Optimism*, (Bantam) 1994

Tolkein, J R R, *The Hobbit,* (Harper Collins) 2013

Tolkein, J R R, *The Lord of the Rings*, (Harper Collins) 2013

Tyler, Richard, *Jolt: Shake Up Your Thinking and Upgrade Your Impact for Extraordinary Success*, (Capstone) 2015

Vignerhoets, Ad, *Why Only Humans Weep: Unravelling the Mysteries of Tears,* (OUP Oxford) 2013

Websites

Kalim, Kessar, (TopTalk), Kessar Kalim, *Director of HR at London School of Hygiene & Tropical Medicine,* https://grosum.com/topTalk/kessar-performance-management/ 6/05/2022

Myatt, Mike, (Forbes), *5 Keys of Dealing with Workplace Conflict*, https://www.forbes.com/sites/mikemyatt/2012/02/22/5-keys-to-dealing-with-workplace-conflict/?sh=1167a5bd1e95 29/01/2021

Rohn, Jim, (Quote-fancy), *Jim Rohn Quotes, https://quotefancy.com/quote/837910/Jim-Rohn-The-same-wind-blows-on-us-all-the-winds-of-disaster-opportunity-and-change 15/10/2022*

Tuazon, Bernie, (Pragmatic Leadership) *Pragmatic Leadership,* https://pragmaticleadership. wordpress.com/ 6/05/2020

Course

Carnegie,Dale *Management Seminar,* 1986

Acknowledgements

Ladey Adey (LA Publications)
For showing me how to get my ideas into a BOOK!

Apple Video
For James who has the patience of Job, and Paul for your skills.

Sue Crooks SJC Marketing
For designing and updating my website and keeping me focused on the future.

Clare Morgan
For having the patience to proof read this book with all its exclamation marks!

John Cleary
For producing such wonderful brand photographs.

Stella Munro
For writing my Obituary/About the Author and making me laugh.

Susan Ogden
For always supporting me with encouragement, space, time, love and understanding.

Tracy Poskitt
For giving me belief.

Richard Tyler
For the fabulous Foreword and your courage.

Vicky, Teresa, Ali and Mark
For always being there.

Ziggi and Dad
Who always watch over me.

Mum
For all your love and support.

Dale Carnegie
William C Byham and Jeff Cox
For inspiring me with their principles and wisdom on dealing with people and business in a humanitarian way.

Chris Brindley MBE
Sandra Garlick MBE
Dr Elena Liquete
For your fabulous endorsements and support

Julie Blant
Martin Cahill
Alastair Cameron
Sally Forgham
Karen Flannery
Wendy Halliday
Jess Jackson
Billy McClung
Mo Pemberton
Dan Roberts
Sarah Thompson
Baz Wright
For your contributions to this book

Kat Derbyshire
Kate Finlay
Sarah Holdsworth
Liz Horsey
Claire Mitton
For your feedback and encouragement.

Index

Sue, Keynote Speaking

Your Notes and Thoughts

Here are some additional pages for you to make notes and add your thoughts as you go through the book and watch the videos.

Your Thoughts

Your Notes and Thoughts

Your Notes and Thoughts

Can I Have A Word?

Your Notes and Thoughts

Your Notes and Thoughts

Lightning Source UK Ltd.
Milton Keynes UK
UKHW010622050123
414865UK00002B/267